Satiro-Mastix by Thomas [

or, The Untrussing of the Humorous Poet

Thomas Dekker was a playwright, pamphleteer and poet who, perhaps, deserves greater recognition than he has so far gained.

Despite the fact only perhaps twenty of his plays were published, and fewer still survive, he was far more prolific than that. Born around 1572 his peak years were the mid 1590's to the 1620's – seven of which he spent in a debtor's prison. His works span the late Elizabethan and Caroline eras and his numerous collaborations with Ford, Middleton, Webster and Jonson say much about his work.

His pamphlets detail much of the life in these times, times of great change, of plague and of course that great capital city London a swirling mass of people, power, intrigue.

Index of Contents

Dramatis Personæ
William Rufus.
Sir Walter Terill.

Sir Rees ap Vaughan.
Sir. Quintilian Shorthose.
Sir Adam Prickshaft.
Blunt.
Crispinus.
Demetrius Fannius.
Tucca.
Horace.
Asinius Bubo.
Peter Flash.
Cælestine.
Mistris Miniver.
Ladies:- Petula, Dicache, Philocalia

Ad Detractorem.

Non potes in Nugas dicere plura meas,
Jpse ego quam dixi.—Qui se mirantur, in illos
Virus habe: Nos hæc nouimus esse nihil.

To the World

World, I was once resolu'd to bee round with thee, because I know tis thy fashion to bee round with euery bodie: but the winde shifting his point, the Veine turn'd: yet because thou wilt sit as Judge of all matters (though for thy labour thou wear'st Midasses eares, and art Monstrum horrendum, informe: Ingens cui lumen ademptum; whose great Poliphemian eye is put out) I care not much if I make description (before thy Vniuersality) of that terrible Poetomachia, lately commenc'd betweene Horace the second, and a band of leane-witted Poetasters. They haue bin at high wordes, and so high, that the ground could not serue them, but (for want of Chopins) haue stalk't vpon Stages.

Horace hal'd his Poetasters to the Barre, the Poetasters vntruss'd Horace: how worthily eyther, or how wrongfully, (World) leaue it to the Jurie: Horace (questionles) made himselfe beleeue, that his Burgonian wit might desperately challenge all commers, and that none durst take vp the foyles against him: It's likely. if he had not so beleiu'd, he had not bin so deceiu'd, for hee was answer'd at his owne weapon: And if before Apollo himselfe (who is Coronator Poetarum) an Inquisition should be taken touching this lamentable merry murdering of Innocent Poetry: all mount Helicon to Bun-hill, it would be found on the Poetasters side Se defendendo. Notwithstanding the Doctors thinke otherwise. I meete one, and he runnes full Butt at me with his Satires hornes, for that in vntrussing Horace, I did onely whip his fortunes, and condition of life, where the more noble Reprehension had bin of his minds Deformitie, whose greatnes if his Criticall Lynx had with as narrow eyes, obseru'd in himselfe, as it did little spots vpon others, without all disputation: Horace would not haue left Horace out of Euery man in's Hvmour. His fortunes? why does not he taxe that onely in others? Read his Arraignement and see. A second Cat-a-mountaine mewes, and calles me Barren, because my braines could bring foorth no other Stigmaticke than Tucca, whome Horace had put to making, and begot to my hand: but I wonder what language

Tucca would haue spoke, if honest Capten Hannam had bin borne without a tongue? Ist not as lawfull then for mee to imitate Horace, as Horace Hannam?

Besides, If I had made an opposition of any other new-minted fellow, (of what Test so euer) hee had bin out-fac'd, and out-weyed by a settled former approbation: neyther was it much improper to set the same dog vpon Horace, whom Horace had set to worrie others.

I could heere (eeuen with the feather of my pen) wipe off other ridiculous imputations: but my best way to answer them, is to laugh at them: onely thus much I protest (and sweare by the diuinest part of true Poesie) that (howsoeuer the limmes of my naked lines may bee and I know haue bin, tortur'd on the racke) they are free from conspiring the least disgrace to any man, but onely to our new Horace; neyther should this ghost of Tucca, haue walkt vp and downe Poules Church-yard, but that hee was raiz'd vp (in print) by newe Exorcismes. World, if thy Hugenes will beleiue this: doe, if not, I care not: for I dedicate my booke not to thy Greatnes, but to the Greatnes of thy scorne: Defying which, let that mad Dog Detraction bite till his teeth bee worne to the stumps: Enuy feede thy Snakes so fat with poyson till they burst: World, let all thy Adders shoote out their Hidra-headed-forked Stinges, Ha, Ha, Nauci; if none will take my part, (as I desire none) yet I thanke thee (thou true Venusian Horace) for these good wordes thou giu'st me: Populus me sibylat at mihi plaudo.

World farewell.

Malim Conuiuis quam placuisse Cocis.

Ad Lectorem

In steed of the Trumpets sounding thrice, before the Play begin: it shall not be amisse (for him that will read) first to beholde this short Comedy of Errors, and where the greatest enter, to giue them in stead of a hisse, a gentle correction.

In letter C. Page. I. for, Whom I adorn'd as Subiects: Read, Whom I ador'd as, &c.

In Letter C Pa. 3. for, Ile starte thence poore: Read, Ile starue their poore, &c.

In Letter C Pa. 6. for, her white cheekes with her dregs and bottome: Read, her white cheekes with the dregs and, &c.

In the same Page, for, Strike off the head of Sin: Read, Strike off the swolne head, &c.

In the same Page, for, that of fiue hundred, foure hundred fiue Read, that of fiue hundred: foure.

In Letter G. pa. 1. for, this enterchanging of languages: Read, this enterchange of language.

In Letter L. pa. 5 for, And stinging insolence should: Read, And stinking insolence, &c.

ACT I

SCENE I. A Room in the House of Sir Quintilian Shorthose

Enter two GENTLEWOMEN strewing of flowers.

1st GENTLEWOMEN
Come bedfellow come, strew apace, strew, strew: in good troth tis pitty that these flowers must be trodden vnder feete as they are like to bee anon.

2nd GENTLEWOMEN
Pitty, alacke pretty heart, thou art sorry to see any good thing fall to the ground: pitty? no more pitty, then to see an Innocent Maydenhead deliuered vp to the ruffling of her new-wedded husband. Beauty is made for vse, and hee that will not vse a sweete soule well, when she is vnder his fingers, I pray Venus he may neuer kisse a faire and a delicate, soft, red, plump-lip.

1st GENTLEWOMEN
Amen, and that's torment enough.

2nd GENTLEWOMEN
Pitty? come foole, fling them about lustily; flowers neuer dye a sweeter death, than when they are smoother'd to death in a Louers bosome, or else paue the high wayes, ouer which these pretty, simpring, setting things, call'd brides, must trippe.

1st GENTLEWOMEN
I pray thee tell mee, why doe they vse at weddings to furnish all places thus, with sweet hearbes and flowers?

2nd GENTLEWOMEN
One reason is, because tis—ô a most sweet thing to lye with a man.

1st GENTLEWOMEN
I thinke tis a O more more more more sweet to lye with a woman.

2nd GENTLEWOMEN
I warrant all men are of thy minde: another reason is, because they sticke like the scutchions of madame chastity, on the sable ground, weeping in their stalkes, and wincking with theyr yellow-sunke eyes, as loath to beholde the lamentable fall of a Maydenhead: what senceles thing in all the house, that is not nowe as melancholy, as a new set-vp Schoolemaster?

1st GENTLEWOMEN
Troth I am.

2nd GENTLEWOMEN

Troth I thinke thou mournst, because th'ast mist thy turne, I doe by the quiuer of Cupid: you see the torches melt themselues away in teares: the instruments weare theyr heart stringes out for sorrow: and the Siluer Ewers weepe most pittifull Rosewater: fiue or sixe payre of the white innocent wedding gloues, did in my sight choose rather to be torne in peeces than to be drawne on; and looke this Rosemary, (a fatall hearbe) this dead-mans nose-gay, has crept in amongst these flowers to decke th' inuisible coarse of the Brides Maydenhead, when (oh how much do we poore wenches suffer) about eleuen or twelue, or one a clock at midnight at furthest, it descends to purgatory, to giue notice that Cælestine (hey ho) will neuer come to lead Apes in hell.

1st GENTLEWOMEN
I see by thy sighing thou wilt not.

2nd GENTLEWOMEN
If I had as many Mayden-heads, as I have hayres on my head, Ide venture them all rather then to come into so hot a place; prethy strew thou, for my little armes are weary.

1st GENTLEWOMEN
I am sure thy little tongue is not.

2nd GENTLEWOMEN
No faith that's like a woman bitten tw fleas, it neuer lyes stil: fye vpont, what a miserable thing tis to be a noble Bride, there's such delayes in rising, in fitting gownes, in tyring, in pinning Rebatoes, in poaking, in dinner, in supper, in Reuels, & last of all in cursing the poore nodding fidlers, for keeping Mistris Bride so long vp from sweeter Reuels; that, oh I could neuer endure to put it vp without much bickering.

1st GENTLEWOMEN
Come th'art an odde wench, hark, harke, musicke? nay then the Bride's vp.

2nd GENTLEWOMEN
Is she vp? nay then I see she has been downe: Lord ha mercy on vs, we women fall and fall still, and when we haue husbands we play upon them like Virginall Jackes, they must ryse and fall to our humours, or else they'l neuer get any good straines of musicke out of vs; but come now, haue at it for a mayden-head.

Strew.

As they strew, enter SIR QUINTILIAN SHORTHOSE with PETER FLASH and two or three Seruingmen, with lights.

SIR QUINTILIAN SHORTHOSE
Come knaues, night begins to be like my selfe, an olde man; day playes the theefe and steales vpon vs; O well done wenches, well done, well done, you haue couered all the stony way to church with flowers, tis well, tis well, ther's an Embleame too, to be made out of these flowers and stones, but you are honest wenches, in, in, in.

2nd GENTLEWOMEN
When we come to your yeares, we shal learne what honesty is, come pew-fellow.

Exeunt.

SIR QUINTILIAN SHORTHOSE
Is the musicke come yet? so much to do! Ist come?

OMNES
Come sir.

SIR QUINTILIAN SHORTHOSE
Haue the merry knaues pul'd their fiddle cases ouer their
instruments eares?

FLASH
As soone as ere they entred our gates, the noyse went, before they came nere the great Hall, the faint
hearted villiacoes sounded at least thrice.

SIR QUINTILIAN SHORTHOSE
Thou shouldst haue reuiu'd them with a Cup of burnt wine and sugar; sirra, you, horse-keeper, goe, bid
them curry theyr strings: Is my daughter vp yet?

Exit.

FLASH
Vp sir? she was seene vp an houre agoe.

SIR QUINTILIAN SHORTHOSE
Shee's an early sturrer, ah sirra.

FLASH
Shee'l be a late sturrer soone at night sir.

SIR QUINTILIAN SHORTHOSE
Goe too Peter Flash, you haue a good sodaine flash of braine, your wittes husky, and no maruaile, for tis
like one of our Comedians beardes, still ith stubble: about your busines, and looke you be nymble to flye
from the wine, or the nymble wine will catch you by the nose.

FLASH
If your wine play with my nose Sir, Ile knocke's coxcombe.

SIR QUINTILIAN SHORTHOSE
Doe Peeter, and weare it for thy labour;
Is my Sonne in Law Sir Walter Terell ready yet?

OMNES
Ready sir.

Exit ANOTHER

SIR QUINTILIAN SHORTHOSE
One of you attend him: Stay Flash, where's the note of the guestes you haue inuited?

FLASH
Here Sir, Ile pull all your guestes out of my bosome; the men that will come, I haue crost, but all the Gentlewomen haue at the tayle of the last letter a pricke, because you may read them the better.

SIR QUINTILIAN SHORTHOSE
My spectacles, lyght, lyght, knaues:
Sir Adam Prickshaft, thou hast crost him, heele come.

FLASH
I had much a doe sir, to draw Sir Adam Prickeshaft home, because I tolde him twas early, but heele come.

SIR QUINTILIAN SHORTHOSE
Justice Crop, what will he come?

FLASH
He took phisicke yesterday sir.

SIR QUINTILIAN SHORTHOSE
Oh then Crop cannot come.

FLASH
O Lord yes, sir yes, twas but to make more roome in his
Crop for your good cheare, Crop will come.

SIR QUINTILIAN SHORTHOSE
Widdow Mineuer.

FLASH
Shee's prickt you see sir, and will come.

SIR QUINTILIAN SHORTHOSE
Sir Vaughan ap Rees, oh hee's crost twise, so, so, so, then all these Ladyes, that fall downewardes heere, will come I see, and all these Gentlemen that stand right before them.

FLASH
All wil come.

SIR QUINTILIAN SHORTHOSE
Well sayd, heere, wryte them out agen, and put the men from the women, and Peeter, when we are at Church bring wine and cakes, be light & nimble good Flash, for your burden will be but light.

Enter SIR ADAM a light before him.

Sir Adam Prickeshaft.

God morrow, god morrow: goe, in, in, in, to the
Bridegroome, taste a cup of burnt wine this morning, twill make
you flye the better all the day after.

SIR ADAM
You are an early styrrer Sir Quintilian Shorthose.

SIR QUINTILIAN SHORTHOSE
I am so, it behoues me at my daughters wedding, in, in, in; fellow put out thy torch, and put thy selfe
into my buttery, the torch burnes ill in thy hand, the wine will burne better in thy belly, in, in.

FLASH
Ware there, roome for Sir Adam Prickeshaft: your Worship—

Exit.

Enter SIR VAUGHAN and MISTRIS MINEUER.

SIR QUINTILIAN SHORTHOSE
Sir Vaughan and Widdow Mineuer, welcome, welcome, a thousand times: my lips Mistris Widdow shall
bid you God morrow, in, in, one to the Bridegroome, the other to the Bride.

SIR VAUGHAN
 Why then Sir quiontilian Shorthose, I will step into mistris Bride, and Widdow Mineuer, shall goe vpon
M. Bridegroome.

MISTRIS MINIVER
No pardon, for by my truely Sir Vaughan, Ile ha no dealings with any M. Bridegroomes.

SIR QUINTILIAN SHORTHOSE
In widdow in, in honest knight in.

SIR VAUGHAN
I will vsher you mistris widdow.

FLASH
Light there for Sir Vaughan; your good Worship—

SIR VAUGHAN
Drinke that shilling Ma. Peter Flash, in your guttes and belly.

FLASH
Ile not drinke it downe sir, but Ile turne it into that which shall run downe, oh merrily!

Exit SIR VAUGHAN

Enter BLUNT, CRISPINUS, DEMETRIUS, and others with Ladies, lights before them.

SIR QUINTILIAN SHORTHOSE
God morrow to these beauties, and Gentlemen, that haue Vshered this troope of Ladyes to my daughters wedding, welcome, welcome all; musick? nay then the bridegroome's comming, where are these knaues heere?

FLASH
All here sir.

Enter TERRILL, SIR ADAM, SIR VAUGHAN, CELESTINE, MISTRIS MINEUER and other Ladies and attendants with lights.

TERRILL
God morrow Ladies and fayre troopes of gallants, that haue depos'd the drowzy King of sleep, to Crowne our traine with your rich presences, I salute you all;

Each one share thanks from thanks in generall.

CRISPINUS
God morrow M. Bride-groome, mistris Bride.

OMNES
God morrow M. Bride-groome.

TERRILL
Gallants I shal intreate you to prepare,
For Maskes and Reuels to defeate the night,
Our Soueraigne will in person grace our marriage.

SIR QUINTILIAN SHORTHOSE
What will the king be heer?

TERRILL
Father he will.

SIR QUINTILIAN SHORTHOSE
Where be these knaues? More Rose-mary and gloues, gloues, gloues: choose Gentlemen; Ladyes put on soft skins vpon the skin of softer hands; so, so: come mistris Bride take you your place, the olde men first, and then the Batchelors; Maydes with the Bride, Widdows and wiues together, the priest's at Church, tis time that we march thether.

TERRILL
Deare Blunt at our returne from Church, take paines to step to Horace, for our nuptiall songs; now Father when you please.

SIR QUINTILIAN SHORTHOSE
Agreed, set on, come good Sir Vaughan, must we lead the way?

SIR VAUGHAN

Peeter you goe too fast for Mistris pride: so, gingerly,
gingerly; I muse why Sir Adam Prickeshaft sticks so short behinde?

SIR QUINTILIAN SHORTHOSE
He follows close, not too fast, holde vp knaues,
Thus we lead youth to church, they vs to graues.

Exeunt.

SCENE II

HORACE sitting in a study behinde a Curtaine, a candle by him burning, bookes lying confusedly: to
himselfe.

HORACE
To thee whose fore-head swels with Roses,
Whose most haunted bower
Giues life & sent to euery flower,
Whose most adored name incloses,
Things abstruse, deep and diuine,
Whose yellow tresses shine,
Bright as Eoan fire.
O me thy Priest inspire.
For I to thee and thine immortall name,
In—in—in golden tunes,
For I to thee and thine immortall name—
In—sacred raptures flowing, flowing, swimming, swimming:
In sacred raptures swimming,
Immortal name, game, dame, tame, lame, lame, lame,
Pux, hath, shame, proclaime, oh—
In Sacred raptures flowing, will proclaime, not—
O me thy Priest inspyre!
For I to thee and thine immortall name,
In flowing numbers fild with spright and flame,
Good, good, in flowing numbers fild with spright & flame.

Enter ASINIUS BUBO.

ASINIUS BUBO
Horace, Horace, my sweet ningle, is alwayes in labour when I come, the nine Muses be his midwiues I
pray Jupiter: Ningle.

HORACE
In flowing numbers fild with sprite and flame,
To thee.

ASINIUS BUBO
To me? I pledge thee sweet Ningle, by Bacchus quaffing boule, I thought th'adst drunke to me.

HORACE
It must haue been in the deuine lycour of Pernassus, then in
which, I know you would scarce haue pledg'd me, but come sweet roague,
sit, sit, sit.

ASINIUS BUBO
Ouer head and eares yfaith? I haue a sacke-full of newes for thee, thou shalt plague some of them, if
God send vs life and health together.

HORACE
Its no matter, empty thy sacke anon, but come here first honest roague, come.

ASINIUS BUBO
Ist good, Ist good, pure Helicon ha?

HORACE
Dam me ift be not the best that euer came from me, if I haue any iudgement, looke sir, tis an
Epithalamium for Sir Walter Terrels wedding, my braines haue giuen assault to it but this morning.

ASINIUS BUBO
Then I hope to see them flye out like gun-powder ere night.

HORACE
Nay good roague marke, for they are the best lynes that euer I drew.

ASINIUS BUBO
Heer's the best leafe in England, but on, on, Ile but tune this Pipe.

HORACE
Marke, to thee whose fore-head swels with Roses.

ASINIUS BUBO
O sweet, but will there be no exceptions taken, because fore-head and swelling comes together?

HORACE
Push away, away, its proper, besides tis an elegancy to say the fore head swels.

ASINIUS BUBO
Nay an't be proper, let it stand for Gods loue.

HORACE
Whose most haunted bower,
Giues life and sent to euery flower,
Whose most adored name incloses,
Things abstruse, deep and diuine.

Whose yellow tresses shine,
Bright as Eoan fire.

ASINIUS BUBO
O pure, rich, ther's heate in this, on, on.

HORACE
Bright as Eoan fire,
O me thy Priest inspire!
For I to thee and thine immortall name—marke this.
In flowing numbers fild with spryte and flame.

ASINIUS BUBO
I mary, ther's spryte and flame in this.

HORACE
A pox, a this Tobacco.

ASINIUS BUBO
Wod this case were my last, if I did not marke, nay all's
one, I haue alwayes a consort of Pypes about me, myne Ingle is all fire
and water; I markt, by this Candle (which is none of Gods Angels) I
remember, you started back at sprite and flame.

HORACE
For I to thee and thine immortall name,
In flowing numbers fild with sprite and flame,
To thee Loues mightiest King,
Himen ô Himen, does our chaste Muse sing.

ASINIUS BUBO
Ther's musicke in this.

HORACE
Marke now deare Asinius.
Let these virgins quickly see thee,
Leading out the Bride,
Though theyr blushing cheekes they hide,
Yet with kisses will they fee thee,
To vntye theyr Virgin zone,
They grieue to lye alone.

ASINIUS BUBO
So doe I by Venus.

HORACE
Yet with kisses wil they fee thee, my Muse has marcht (deare roague) no farder yet: but how ist? how
ist? nay prethee good Asinius deale plainly, doe not flatter me, come, how?—

ASINIUS BUBO
If I haue any iudgement:

HORACE
Nay look you Sir, and then follow a troope of other rich and labour'd conceipts, oh the end shall be admirable! but how ist sweet Bubo, how, how?

ASINIUS BUBO
If I have any Iudgement, tis the best stuffe that euer dropt from thee.

HORACE
You ha seene my Acrosticks?

ASINIUS BUBO
Ile put vp my pypes and then Ile see any thing.

HORACE
Th'ast a Coppy of mine Odes to, hast not Bubo?

ASINIUS BUBO
Your odes? O that which you spake by word a mouth at th' ordinary, when Musco the gull cryed Mew at it.

HORACE
A pox on him poore braineles Rooke: and you remember, I tolde him his wit lay at pawne with his new Sattin sute, and both would be lost, for not fetching home by a day.

ASINIUS BUBO
At which he would faine ha blusht but that his painted cheekes would not let him.

HORACE
Nay sirra the Palinode, which I meane to stitch to my Reuels, shall be the best and ingenious peece that euer I swet for; stay roague, Ile fat thy spleane and make it plumpe with laughter.

ASINIUS BUBO
Shall I? fayth Ningle, shall I see thy secrets?

HORACE
Puh my friends.

ASINIUS BUBO
But what fardle's that? what fardle's that?

HORACE
Fardle, away, tis my packet; heere lyes intoomb'd the loues of Knights and Earles, heere tis, heere tis, heere tis, Sir Walter Terils letter to me, and my answere to him: I no sooner opened his letter, but there appeared to me three glorious Angels, whome I ador'd as subiectes doe their Soueraignes: the honest

knight Angles for my acquaintance, with such golden baites— but why doost laugh my good roague? how is my answere, prethee, how, how?

ASINIUS BUBO
Answere, as God iudge me Ningle, for thy wit thou mayst answer any Iustice of peace in England I warrant; thou writ'st in a most goodly big hand too, I like that, & readst as leageably as some that haue bin sau'd by their neck-verse.

HORACE
But how dost like the Knights inditing?

ASINIUS BUBO
If I haue any iudgement; a pox ont, heer's worshipfull lynes indeed, heer's stuffe: but sirra Ningle, of what fashion is this knights wit, of what blocke?

HORACE
Why you see; wel, wel, an ordinary Ingenuity, a good wit for a knight, you know how, before God I am haunted with some the most pittyfull dry gallants.

ASINIUS BUBO
Troth so I think; good peeces of lantskip, shew best a far off.

HORACE
I, I, I, excellent sumpter horses, carry good cloaths; but honest roague, come, what news, what newes abroad? I haue heard a the horses walking a' th top of Paules.

ASINIUS BUBO
Ha ye? why the Captain Tucca rayles vpon you most preposterously behinde your backe, did you not heare him?

HORACE
A pox vpon him: by the white & soft hand of Minerua, Ile make him the most ridiculous: dam me if I bring not's humor ath stage: &—scuruy lymping tongu'd captaine, poor greasie buffe Ierkin, hang him: tis out of his Element to traduce me: I am too well ranckt Asinius to bee stab'd with his dudgion wit: sirra, Ile compose an Epigram vpon him, shall goe thus—

ASINIUS BUBO
Nay I ha more news, ther's Crispinus & his Iorneyman Poet Demetrius Faninus too, they sweare they'll bring your life & death vpon'th stage like a Bricklayer in a play.

HORACE
Bubo they must presse more valiant wits than theyr own to do it: me ath stage? ha, ha. Ile starue their poore copper-lace workmasters, that dare play me: I can bring (& that they quake at) a prepar'd troope of gallants, who for my sake shal distaste euery vnsalted line, in their fly-blowne Comedies.

ASINIUS BUBO
Nay that's certaine, ile bring 100. gallants of my ranke.

HORACE
That same Crispinus is the silliest Dor, and Faninus the slightest cob-web-lawne peece of a Poet, oh God!

Why should I care what euery Dor doth buz
In credulous eares, it is a crowne to me,
That the best iudgements can report me wrong'd.

ASINIUS BUBO
I am one of them that can report it.

HORACE
I thinke but what they are, and am not moou'd.
The one a light voluptuous Reueler,
The other, a strange arrogating puffe,
Both impudent, and arrogant enough.

ASINIUS BUBO
S'lid do not Criticus Reuel in these lynes, ha Ningle ha?

[Knocking.

HORACE
Yes, they're mine owne.

CRISPINUS
Horrace.

DEMETRIUS
Flaccus.

CRISPINUS
Horrace, not vp yet.

HORACE
Peace, tread softly, hyde my Papers; who's this so early?
Some of my rookes, some of my guls?

CRISPINUS
Horrace, Flaccus.

HORACE
Who's there? stray, treade softly: Wat Terill on my life: who's there? my gowne sweete roague, so,
come vp, come in.

Enter CRISPINUS and DEMETRIUS.

CRISPINUS
God morrow Horrace.

HORACE
O, God saue you gallants.

CRISPINUS
Asinius Bubo well met.

ASINIUS BUBO
Nay, I hope so Crispinus, yet I was sicke a quarter of a yeare a goe of a vehement great tooth-atch: a pox ont, it bit me vilye, as God sa me la I knew twas you by your knocking so soone as I saw you; Demetrius Fannius, wil you take a whiffe this morning? I haue tickling geare now, heer's that will play with your nose, and a pype of mine owne scowring too.

DEMETRIUS
I, and a Hodgshead too of your owne, but that will neuer be scowred cleane I feare.

ASINIUS BUBO
I burnt my pype yesternight, and twas neuer vsde since, if you will tis at your seruice gallants, and Tobacco too, tis right pudding I can tell you; a Lady or two, tooke a pype full or two at my hands, and praizde it for the Heauens, shall I fill Flannius?

DEMETRIUS
I thanke you good Asinius for your loue,
I sildome take that Phisicke, tis enough
Hauing so much foole to take him in snuffe.

HORACE
Good Bubo read some booke, and giue vs leaue....

ASINIUS BUBO
Leaue haue you deare Ningle, marry for reading any book Ile take my death vpont (as my Ningle sayes) tis out of my Elemēt: no faith, euer since I felt one hit me ith teeth that the greatest Clarkes are not the wisest men, could I abide to goe to Schoole, I was at As in presenti and left there: yet because Ile not be counted a worse foole then I am, Ile turne ouer a new leafe.

Asinius reads and takes Tabacco.

HORACE
To see my fate, that when I dip my pen
In distilde Roses, and doe striue to dreine,
Out of myne Inke all gall; that when I wey
Each sillable I write or speake, because
Mine enemies with sharpe and searching eyes
Looke through & through me, caruing my poore labours
Like an Anotomy: Oh heauens to see,
That when my lines are measur'd out as straight
As euen Paralels, tis strange that still,
Still some imagine they are drawne awry.

The error is not mine, but in theyr eye,
That cannot take proportions.

CRISPINUS
Horrace, Horrace,
To stand within the shot of galling tongues,
Proues not your gilt, for could we write on paper,
Made of these turning leaues of heauen, the cloudes,
Or speake with Angels tongues: yet wise men know,
That some would shake the head, tho Saints should sing,
Some snakes must hisse, because they're borne with stings.

HORACE
Tis true.

CRISPINUS
Doe we not see fooles laugh at heauen? and mocke
The Makers workmanship; be not you grieu'd
If that which you molde faire, vpright and smooth,
Be skrwed awry, made crooked, lame and vile,
By racking coments, and calumnious tongues,
So to be bit it rankcles not: for innocence
May with a feather brush off the foulest wrongs.
But when your dastard wit will strike at men
In corners, and in riddles folde the vices
Of your best friends, you must not take to heart,
If they take off all gilding from their pilles,
And onely offer you the bitter Coare.

HORACE
Crispinus.

CRISPINUS
Say that you haue not sworne vnto your Paper,
To blot her white cheekes with the dregs and bottome
Of your friends priuate vices: say you sweare
Your loue and your aleageance to bright vertue
Makes you descend so low, as to put on
The Office of an Executioner,
Onely to strike off the swolne head of sinne,
Where ere you finde it standing,
Say you sweare;
And make damnation parcell of your oath,
That when your lashing iestes make all men bleed;
Yet you whip none. Court, Citty, country, friends,
Foes, all must smart alike; yet Court, nor Citty,
Nor foe, nor friend, dare winch at you; great pitty.

DEMETRIUS
If you sweare, dam me Faninus, or Crispinus,
Or to the law (Our kingdomes golden chaine)
To Poets dam me, or to Players dam me,
If I brand you, or you, tax you, scourge you:
I wonder then, that of fiue hundred: foure
Should all point with their fingers in one instant
At one and the same man?

HORACE
Deare Faninus.

DEMETRIUS
Come, you cannot excuse it.

HORACE
Heare me, I can—

DEMETRIUS
You must daube on thicke collours then to hide it.

CRISPINUS
We come like your Phisitions, to purge
Your sicke and daungerous minde of her disease.

DEMETRIUS
In troth we doe, out of our loues we come,
And not reuenge, but if you strike vs still,
We must defend our reputations:
Our pens shall like our swords be alwayes sheath'd,
Vnlesse too much prouockt, Horace if then
They draw bloud of you, blame vs not, we are men:
Come, let thy Muse beare vp a smoother sayle,
Tis the easiest and the basest Arte to raile.

HORACE
Deliuer me your hands, I loue you both,
As deare as my owne soule, prooue me, and when
I shall traduce you, make me the scorne of men.

BOTH
Enough, we are friends.

CRISPINUS
What reads Asinius?

ASINIUS BUBO
By my troth heer's an excellent comfortable booke, it's most sweet reading in it.

DEMETRIUS
Why, what does it smell of Bubo?

ASINIUS BUBO
Mas it smels of Rose-leaues a little too.

HORACE
Then it must needs be a sweet booke, he would faine perfume his ignorance.

ASINIUS BUBO
I warrant he had wit in him that pen'd it.

CRISPINUS
Tis good yet a foole will confesse truth.

ASINIUS BUBO
The whoorson made me meete with a hard stile in two or three places as I went ouer him.

DEMETRIUS
I beleeue thee, for they had need to be very lowe & easie
Stiles of wit that thy braines goe ouer.

Enter BLUNT and TUCCA.

BLUNT
Wher's this gallant? Morrow Gentlemen: what's this deuise done yet Horace?

HORACE
Gods so, what meane you to let this fellow dog you into my Chamber?

BLUNT
Oh, our honest Captayne, come, prethee let vs see.

TUCCA
Why you bastards of nine whoores, the Muses, why doe you walk heere in this gorgeous gailery of gallant inuentions, with that whooreson poore lyme & hayre-rascall? why—

CRISPINUS
O peace good Tucca, we are all sworne friends.

TUCCA
Sworne, that Iudas yonder that walkes in Rug, will dub you Knights ath Poste, if you serue vnder his band of oaths, the copper-fact rascal wil for a good supper out sweare twelue dozen of graund Iuryes.

BLUNT
A pox ont, not done yet, and bin about it three dayes?

HORACE
By Iesu within this houre, saue you Captayne Tucca.

TUCCA
Dam thee, thou thin bearded Hermaphrodite, dam thee, Ile saue my selfe for one I warrant thee, is this thy Tub Diogines?

HORACE
Yes Captaine this is my poore lodging.

ASINIUS BUBO
Morrow Captaine Tucca, will you whiffe this morning?

TUCCA
Art thou there goates pizzel; no godamercy Caine I am for no whiffs I, come hether sheep-skin-weauer, s'foote thou lookst as though th'adst beg'd out of a layle: drawe, I meane not thy face (for tis not worth drawing) but drawe neere: this way, martch, follow your commaunder you scoundrell: So, thou must run of an errand for mee Mephostophiles.

HORACE
To doe you pleasure Captayne I will, but whether.

TUCCA
To hell, thou knowst the way, to hell my fire and brimstone, to hell; dost stare my Sarsens-head at Newgate? dost gloate? Ile march through thy dunkirkes guts for shooting iestes at me.

HORACE
Deare Captaine but one word.

TUCCA
Out bench-whistler out, ile not take thy word for a dagger Pye: you browne-bread-mouth stinker, ile teach thee to turne me into Bankes his horse, and to tell gentlemen I am a Iugler, and can shew trickes.

HORACE
Captaine Tucca, but halfe a word in your eare.

TUCCA
No you staru'd rascal, thou't bite off mine eares then, you must haue three or foure suites of names, when like a lowsie Pediculous vermin th'ast but one suite to thy backe: you must be call'd Asper, and Criticus, and Horace, thy tytle's longer a reading then the Stile a the big Turkes: Asper, Criticus, Quintus, Horatius, Flaccus.

HORACE
Captaine I know vpon what euen bases I stand, and therefore—

TUCCA
Bases? wud the roague were but ready for me.

BLUNT
Nay prethee deare Tucca, come you shall shake—

TUCCA
Not hands with great Hunkes there, not hands, but Ile shake the gull-groper out of his tan'd skinne.

CRISPINUS & DEMETRIUS
For our sake Captaine, nay prethee holde.

TUCCA
Thou wrongst heere a good honest rascall Crispinus, and a poore varlet Demetrius Fanninus (bretheren in thine owne trade of Poetry) thou sayst Crispinus Sattin dublet is Reauel'd out heere, and that this penurious sneaker is out at elboes, goe two my good full-mouth'd ban-dog, Ile ha thee friends with both.

HORACE
With all my heart captaine Tucca, and with you too, Ile laye my handes vnder your feete, to keepe them from aking.

OMNES
Can you haue any more?

TUCCA
Saist thou me so, olde Coale? come doo't then; yet tis no matter neither, Ile haue thee in league first with these two rowly powlies: they shal be thy Damons and thou their Pithyasse; Crispinus shall giue thee an olde cast Sattin suite, and Demetrius shall write thee a Scene or two, in one of thy strong garlicke Comedies; and thou shalt take the guilt of conscience for't, and sweare tis thine owne olde lad, tis thine owne: thou neuer yet fels't into the hands of sattin, didst?

HORACE
Neuer Captaine I thanke God.

TUCCA
Goe too, thou shalt now King Gorboduck, thou shalt, because Ile ha thee damn'd, Ile ha thee all in Sattin: Asper, Criticus, Quintus, Horatius, Flaccus, Crispinus shal doo't, thou shalt doo't, heyre apparant of Helicon, thou shalt doo't.

ASINIUS BUBO
Mine Ingle weare an olde cast Sattin suite?

TUCCA
I wafer-face your Ningle.

ASINIUS BUBO
If he carry the minde of a Gentleman, he'll scorne it at's heeles.

TUCCA
Mary muffe, my man a ginger-bread, wilt eate any small coale?

ASINIUS BUBO
No Captaine, wod you should well know it, great coale shall not fill my bellie.

TUCCA
Scorne it, dost scorne to be arrested at one of his olde Suites?

HORACE
No Captaine, Ile weare any thing.

TUCCA
I know thou wilt, I know th'art an honest low minded Pigmey, for I ha seene thy shoulders lapt in a Plaiers old cast Cloake, like a Slie knaue as thou art: and when thou ranst mad for the death of Horatio: thou borrowedst a gowne of Roscius the Stager, (that honest Nicodemus) and sentst it home lowsie, didst not? Responde, didst not?

BLUNT
So, so, no more of this, within this houre—

HORACE
If I can sound retreate to my wits, with whome this leader is in skirmish, Ile end within this houre.

TUCCA
What wut end? wut hang thy selfe now? has he not writ Finis yet Iacke? what will he bee fifteene weekes about this Cockatrices egge too? has hee not cackeld yet? not laide yet?

BLUNT
Not yet, hee sweares hee will within this houre.

TUCCA
His wittes are somewhat hard bound: the Puncke his Muse has sore labour ere the whoore bee deliuered: the poore saffron-cheeke Sun-burnt Gipsie wantes Phisicke; giue the hungrie-face pudding-pye-eater ten Pilles: ten shillings my faire Angelica, they'l make his Muse as yare as a tumbler.

BLUNT
He shall not want for money if heele write.

TUCCA
Goe by Ieronimo, goe by; and heere, drop the ten shillings into this Bason; doe, drop, when Iacke? hee shall call me his Mæcenas: besides, Ile dam vp's Ouen-mouth for rayling at's: So, ist right Iacke? ist sterling? fall off now to the vanward of yonder foure Stinkers, and aske alowde if wee shall goe? the Knight shall defray Iacke, the Knight when it comes to Summa totalis, the Knyght, the Knight.—

BLUNT
Well Gentlemen, we'll leaue you, shall we goe Captaine? Good Horrace make some hast.

HORACE
Ile put on wings.

ASINIUS BUBO
I neuer sawe mine Ingle so dasht in my life before.

CRISPINUS
Yes once Asinius.

ASINIUS BUBO
Mas you say true, hee was dasht worse once going (in a rainy day) with a speech to'th Tilt-yard, by Gods lyd has call'd him names, a dog would not put vp, that had any discreation.

TUCCA
Holde, holde vp thy hand, I ha seene the day thou didst not scorne to holde vp thy golles: ther's a Souldiers Spur-royall, twelue pence: Stay, because I know thou canst not write without quick-siluer; vp agen, this goll agen, I giue thee double presse-money: Stay, because I know thou hast a noble head, ile deuide my Crowne, ô royall Porrex, ther's a teston more; goe, thou and thy Muse munch, doe, munch; come my deare Mandrake, if Skeldring fall not to decay, thou shalt florish: farewell my sweet Amadis de Gaule, farewell.

HORACE
Deare Captaine.

TUCCA
Come Iacke.

DEMETRIUS
Nay Captaine stay, we are of your band.

TUCCA
March faire then.

CRISPINUS
Horace farewell, adue Asinius.

Exeunt.

ASINIUS BUBO
Ningle lets goe to some Tauerne, and dine together, for my stomache rises at this scuruy leather Captaine.

HORACE
No, they haue choakt me with mine owne disgrace,
Which (fooles) ile spit againe euen in your face.

Exeunt.

ACT II

SCENE I. The House of Sir Quintilian Shorthose

Enter SIR QUINTILIAN SHORTHOSE, SIR ADAM, SIR VAUGHAN, MISTRES MINEUR with Seruingmen.

SIR QUINTILIAN SHORTHOSE
Knaues, Varlets, what Lungis, giue me a dozen of stooles there.

SIR VAUGHAN
Sesu plesse vs all in our fiue sences a peece, what meane
yee sir Kintilian Sorthose to stand so much on a dozen stooles, heere
be not preeches inuffe to hyde a dozen stooles, |690| vnlesse you wisse
some of vs preake his sinnes.

SIR QUINTILIAN SHORTHOSE
I say sir Vaughan no shinne shal be broken heer; what
lungis, a chayre with a stronge backe, and a soft bellie, great with
childe, with a cushion for this reuerend Lady.

MISTRIS MINIVER
God neuer gaue me the grace to be a Lady, yet I ha beene worshipt in my conscience to my face a
thousand times, I cannot denye sir Vaughan, but that I haue all implements, belonging to the vocation
of a Lady.

SIR VAUGHAN
I trust mistris Mineuer you haue all a honest oman shud haue?

MISTRIS MINIVER
Yes perdie, as my Coach, and my fan, and a man or two that serue my turne, and other things which Ide
bee loath euery one should see, because they shal not be common, I am in manner of a Lady in one
point.

SIR VAUGHAN
I pray mistris Mineuers, let vs all see that point for our better vnderstanding.

MISTRIS MINIVER
For I ha some thinges that were fetcht (I am sure) as farre as some of the Low Countries, and I payde
sweetly for them too, and theytolde me they were good for Ladies.

SIR QUINTILIAN SHORTHOSE
And much good do't thy good heart faire widdow with them.

MISTRIS MINIVER
I am fayre enough to bee a Widdow, Sir Quintilian.

SIR VAUGHAN

In my soule and conscience, and well fauoured enough to be a Lady: heere is sir Kintilian Sorthose, and heere is sir Adam Prickshaft, a sentleman of a very good braine, and well headed: you see he shootes his bolt sildome, but when Adam lets goe, he hits: and heere is sir Vaughan ap Rees, and I beleeue if God sud take vs all from his mercy, as I hope hee will not yet; we all three loue you, at the bottome of our bellyes, and our hearts: and therefore mistris Mineuer, if you please, you shall be knighted by one of vs, whom you sall desire to put into your deuice and minde.

MISTRIS MINIVER
One I must haue sir Vaughan.

SIR QUINTILIAN SHORTHOSE
And one of vs thou shalt haue widdow.

MISTRIS MINIVER
One I must haue, for now euery one seekes to crow ouer me.

SIR VAUGHAN
By Sesu and if I finde any crowing ouer you, & he were a cocke (come out as farre as in Turkeys country) tis possible to cut his combe off.

MISTRIS MINIVER
I muse why sir Adam Prickshaft flyes so farre from vs.

SIR ADAM
I am in a browne study, my deare, if loue should bee turned into a beast, what beast hee were fit to bee turned into.

SIR QUINTILIAN SHORTHOSE
I thinke Sir Adam an Asse, because of his bearing.

MISTRIS MINIVER
I thinke (sauing your reuerence) Sir Adam a puppy, for a dog is the most louing creature to a christian that is, vnles it be a childe.

SIR ADAM
No, I thinke if loue should bee turn'd away, and goe to serue any beast, it must bee an Ape, and my reason—

SIR VAUGHAN
Sir Adam, an Ape? ther's no more reason in an Ape, than in a very plaine Monkey; for an Ape has no tayle, but we all know, or tis our duty to know, loue has two tailes; In my sudsment, if loue be a beast, that beast is a bunce of Reddis; for a bunce of Reddis is wise meate without Mutton, and so is loue.

MISTRIS MINIVER
Ther's the yawning Captaine (sauing your reuerence that has such a sore mouth) would one day needes perswade me, that loue was a Rebato; and his reason was (sauing your reuerence) that a Rebato was worne out with pinning too often; and so he said loue was.

SIR VAUGHAN
And Master Captaine Tucca sayd wisely too, loue is a Rebato indeede: a Rebato must be poaked; now many women weare Rebatoes, and many that weare Rebatoes—

SIR ADAM
Must be poakt.

SIR VAUGHAN
Sir Adam Prickshaft has hit the cloute.

Musicke.

SIR QUINTILIAN SHORTHOSE
The Musicke speakes to vs, we'll haue a daunce before dinner.

Enter SIR WALTER TERRILL, CELESTINE, BLUNT, CRISPINUS, and DEMETRIUS, euery one with a LADY.

ALL
The King's at hand.

TERRILL
Father the King's at hand.
Musicke talke lowder, that thy siluer voice,
May reach my Soueraignes eares.

SIR VAUGHAN
I pray doe so, Musitions bestir your fingers, that you may haue vs all by the eares.

SIR QUINTILIAN SHORTHOSE
His Grace comes, a Hall varlets, where be my men? blow, blow your colde Trumpets till they sweate; tickle them till they sound agen.

BLUNT
Best goe meete his Grace.

ALL
Agreed.

SIR VAUGHAN
Pray all stand bare, as well men as women: Sir Adam is best you hide your head for feare your wise braines take key-colde: on afore Sir Kintilian; Sentlemen fall in before the Ladyes, in seemely order and fashion; so this is comelye.

Enter Trumpets sounding, they goe to the doore, and meete the KING and his Traine, and whilst the Trumpets sound the KING is welcom'd, kisses the Bride, and honors the Bridegroome in dumbe shew.

KING
Nay if your pleasures shrinke at sight of vs,

We shall repent this labour, Mistris Bride
You that for speaking but one word to day,
Must loose your head at night; you that doe stand
Taking your last leaue of virginity;
You that being well begun, must not be Maide:
Winne you the Ladies, I the men will wooe,
Our selfe will leade my blushing Bride with you.

SIR VAUGHAN
God blesse your Maiesty, and send you to be a long King William Rufus ouer vs, when he sees his times & pleasures.

KING
Wee thanke you good Sir Vaughan, wee will take your meaning not your words.

SIR QUINTILIAN SHORTHOSE
Lowde Musicke there.

SIR VAUGHAN
I am glad your Maiesty will take any thing at my hands; my words I trust in Sesu, are spoken betweene my soule and body together, and haue neither Felonies nor treasons about them, I hope.

KING
Good words Sir Vaughan, I prethee giue vs leaue.

SIR VAUGHAN
Good words sir Vaughan? thats by interpretation in english, you'r best giue good words sir Vaughan: god and his Ansells blesse me, what ayles his maiestye to be so tedious and difficult in his right mindes now, I holde my life that file rascall-rymer Horace hath puzd and puzd aboue a hundred merie tales and lyce, into his great and princely eares: by god and he vse it, his being Phœbus priest cannot saue him, if hee were his Sapline too ide prease vpon his coxcomb: good lord blesse me out of his maiesties celler: King Williams, I hope tis none offences to make a supplication to god a mightie for your long life: for by shesu I haue no meaning in't in all the world, vnles rascalls be here that will haue your grace take shalke for shees, and vnlesse Horace has sent lyce to your maiesty.

KING
Horace, what's he sir Vaughan?

SIR VAUGHAN
As hard-fauourd a fellow as your maiestie has seene in a sommers day: he does pen, an't please your grace, toyes that will not please your grace; tis a Poet, we call them Bardes in our Countrie, singes ballads and rymes, and I was mightie sealous, that his Inke which is blacke and full of gall, had brought my name to your maiestie, and so lifted vp your hye and princely coller.

KING
I neither know that Horace, nor mine anger,
If as thou saist our high and princely choller
Be vp, wee'l tread it downe with daunces; Ladies

Loose not your men; faire measures must be tread,
When by so faire a dauncer you are lead.

SIR VAUGHAN
Mistris Minivuer:

MISTRIS MINIVER
Perdie sir Vaughan I cannot dance.

SIR VAUGHAN
Perdie by this Miniuer cappe, and acording to his masesties leaue too, you sall be put in among theise
Ladies, & daunce ere long I trest in god, the saking of the seetes.

They daunce a straine, and whilst the others keepe on, the KING and CELESTINE stay.

KING
That turne faire Bride shews you must turne at night,
In that sweet daunce which steales away delight.

CELESTINE
Then pleasure is a theife, a fit, a feauer.

KING
True, he's the thiefe, but women the receiuer.

Another change; they fall in, the rest goe on.

KING
This change sweet Maide, saies you must change your life,
As Virgins doe.

CELESTINE
Virgins nere change their life,
She that is wiu'd a maide, is Maide and wife.

KING
But she that dyes a Maide;—

CELESTINE
Thrice happy then.

KING
Leades Apes in hell.

CELESTINE
Better leade Apes then men.

At this third change they end, and she meetes the KING.

KING
Well met.

CELESTINE
Tis ouertaken.

KING
Why faire sweet?

CELESTINE
Women are ouertaken when they meete.

KING
Your bloud speakes like a coward.

CELESTINE
It were good,
If euery Maiden blush, had such a bloud.

KING
A coward bloud, why whom should maidens feare?

CELESTINE
Men, were Maides cowards, they'd not come so nere,
My Lord the Measure's done, I pleade my duetie.

KING
Onelie my heart takes measure of thy beautie.

SIR QUINTILIAN SHORTHOSE
Now by my hose I sweare, that's no deepe oath,
This was a fine sweet earth-quake gentlie moou'd,
By the soft winde of whispring Silkes: come Ladies,
Whose ioynts are made out of the dauncing Orbes,
Come, follow me, walke a colde measure now;
In the Brides Chamber; your hot beautie's melt,
Take euerie one her fan, giue them their places,
And waue the Northerne winde vpon your faces.

CELESTINE and all the Ladyes doing obeysance to the KING, who onely kisses her, Exeunt, SHORTHOSE
manning them, the Gallants stand aloofe.

KING
Sir Walter Terrill.

TERRILL
My confirmed Leige.

KING
Beautie out of her bountie, thee hath lent,
More then her owne with liberall extent.

TERRILL
What meanes my Lord?

KING
Thy Bride, thy choice, thy wife,
She that is now thy fadom, thy new world,
That brings thee people, and makes little subiects;
Kneele at thy feete, obay in euerie thing,
So euerie Father is a priuate King.

TERRILL
My Lord, her beauty is the poorest part,
Chieflie her vertues did endowe my heart.

KING
Doe not back-bite her beauties, they all shine,
Brighter on thee, because the beames are thine,
To thee more faire, to others her two lips
Shew like a parted Moone in thine Eclipse;
That glaunce, which louers mongst themselues deuise,
Walkes as inuisible to others eies:
Giue me thine eare.

CRISPINUS
What meanes the King?

DEMETRIUS
Tis a quaint straine.

TERRILL
My Lord.

KING
Thou darst not Wat.

TERRILL
She is too course an obiect for the Court.

KING
Thou darst not Wat: let to night be to morrow.

TERRILL
For shee's not yet mine owne.

KING
Thou darst not Wat?

TERRILL
My Lord I dare, but—

KING
But I see thou darst not.

TERRILL
This night.

KING
Yea, this night, tush thy minde repaires not,
The more thou talk'st of night, the more thou darst not;
Thus farre I tend, I wod but turne this spheare,
Of Ladies eyes, and place it in the Court,
Where thy faire Bride should for the Zodiacke shine,
And euery Lady else sit for a signe.
But all thy thoughts are yellow, thy sweet bloud
Rebels, th'art iealous Wat; thus with proude reuels
To emmulate the masking firmament,
Where Starres dance in the siluer Hall of heauen,
Thy pleasure should be seasoned, and thy bed
Relish thy Bride, But, but thou darst not Wat.

TERRILL
My Loord I dare.

KING
Speake that agen.

TERRILL
I dare.

KING
Agen kinde Wat, and then I know thou darst.

TERRILL
I dare and will by that ioynt holy oath,
Which she and I swore to the booke of heauen.
This very day when the surueying Sunne,
Riz like a witnes to her faith and mine,
By all the loyalty that subiects owe
To Maiesty, by that, by this, by both,
I sweare to make a double guarded oath,
This night vntainted by the touch of man,

She shall a Virgin come.

KING
To Court?

TERRILL
To Court.
I know I tooke a woman to my wife,
And I know women to be earthly Moones,
That neuer shine till night, I know they change
Their Orbes (their husbands) and in sickish hearts,
Steale to their sweete Endimions, to be cur'd
With better Phisicke, sweeter dyet drinkes,
Then home can minister: all this I know
Yet know not all, but giue me leaue O King,
To boast of mine, and saie that I know none;
I haue a woman but not such a one.

KING
Why, she's confirmed in thee; I now approoue her,
If constant in thy thoughts who then can mooue her?

Enter SIR QUINTILIAN SHORTHOSE

SIR QUINTILIAN SHORTHOSE
Wilt please your Highnes take your place within,
The Ladies attend the Table.

KING
I goe good Knight; Wat thy oath.

TERRILL
My Lord,
My oath's my honour, my honour is my life,
My oath is constant, so I hope my wife.

Exeunt.

SCENE II. Horace's Study

Enter HORACEin his true attyre, ASINIUS BUBO bearing his Cloake.

ASINIUS BUBO
If you flye out Ningle, heer's your Cloake; I thinke it raines too.

HORACE

Hide my shoulders in't.

ASINIUS BUBO
Troth so th'adst neede, for now thou art in thy Pee and Kue; thou hast such a villanous broad backe, that I warrant th'art able to beare away any mans iestes in England.

HORACE
It's well Sir, I ha strength to beare yours mee thinkes; fore God you are growne a piece of a Critist, since you fell into my hands: ah little roague, your wit has pickt vp her crums prettie and well.

ASINIUS BUBO
Yes faith, I finde my wit a the mending hand Ningle; troth I doe not thinke but to proceede Poetaster next Commencement, if I haue my grace perfectlie: euerie one that confer with me now, stop their nose in merriment, and sweare I smell somewhat of Horace; one calles me Horaces Ape, another Horaces Beagle, and such Poeticall names it passes. I was but at Barbers last day, and when he was rencing my face, did but crie out, fellow thou makst me Conniue too long, & sayes he, Master Asinius Bubo, you haue eene Horaces wordes as right as if he had spit them into your mouth.

HORACE
Well, away deare Asinius, deliuer this letter to the young Gallant Druso, he that fell so strongly in loue with mee yesternight.

ASINIUS BUBO
It's a sweete Muske-cod, a pure spic'd-gull; by this feather I pittie his Ingenuities; but hast writ all this since Ningle? I know thou hast a good running head and thou listest.

HORACE
Foh come, your great belly'd wit must long for euery thing too; why you Rooke, I haue a set of letters readie starcht to my hands, which to any fresh suited gallant, that but newlie enters his name into my rowle, I send the next morning, ere his ten a clocke dreame has rize from him, onelie with claping my hand to't, that my Nouice shall start, ho and his haire stand an end, when hee sees the sodaine flash of my writing; what you prettie Diminitiue roague, we must haue false fiers to amaze these spangle babies, these true heires of Ma. Justice Shallow.

ASINIUS BUBO
I wod alwaies haue thee sawce a foole thus.

HORACE
Away, and, stay: heere be Epigrams vpon Tucca, divulge these among the gallants; as for Crispinus, that Crispin-asse and Fannius his Play-dresser; who (to make the Muses beleeue, their subiects eares were staru'd, and that there was a dearth of Poesie) cut an Innocent Moore i'th middle, to serue him in twice; & when he had done, made Poules-worke of it, as for these Twynnes these Poet-apes:
Their Mimicke trickes shall serue
With mirth to feast our Muse, whilst their owne starue.

ASINIUS BUBO
Well Ningle Ile trudge, but where's the Randeuow?

HORACE
Well thought off, marie at Sir Vaughans lodging the Welsh knight, I haue compos'd a loue-letter for the gallants worship, to his Rosamond: the second, Mistris Miniver, because she does not thinke so soundly of his lame English as he could wish; I ha gull'd his Knight-ship heere to his face, yet haue giuen charge to his wincking vnderstanding not to perceiue it: nay Gods so, away deare Bubo.

ASINIUS BUBO
I am gone.

Exit.

HORACE
The Muses birdes the Bees were hiu'd and fled,
Vs in our cradle, thereby prophecying;
That we to learned eares should sweetly sing,
But to the vulger and adulterate braine,
Should loath to prostitute our Virgin straine.
No, our sharpe pen shall keep the world in awe,
Horace thy Poesie, wormwood wreathes shall weare,
We hunt not for mens loues but for their feare.

Exit.

ACT III

SCENE I. The House of Sir Quintilian Shorthose

Enter SIR ADAM and MISTRIS MINIVER.

MISTRIS MINIVER
O Sir Adam Prickshaft, you are a the bow hand wide, a long yard I assure you: and as for Suitors, truelie they all goe downe with me, they haue all one flat answere.

SIR ADAM
All Widdow? not all, let Sir Adam bee your first man still.

Enter SIR QUINTILIAN SHORTHOSE.

SIR QUINTILIAN SHORTHOSE
Widdow, art stolne from Table? I Sir Adam,
Are you my riuall? well, flye faire y'are best;
The King's exceeding merrie at the banquet,
He makes the Bride blush with his merrie words,
That run into her eares; ah he's a wanton,
Yet I dare trust her, had he twentie tongues,
And euerie tongue a Stile of Maiestie.

Now Widdow, let me tell thee in thine eare,
I loue thee Widdow, by this ring; nay weare it.

MISTRIS MINIVER
Ile come in no rings pardie, Ile take no golde.

SIR ADAM
Harke in thine eare, take me, I am no golde.

Enter SIR VAUGHAN and PETER FLASH.

SIR VAUGHAN
Master Peter Flash, I will grope about Sir Quintilian, for his terminations touching and considering you.

FLASH
I thanke your Worship, for I haue as good a stomacke to your
Worship as a man could wish.

SIR VAUGHAN
I hope in God a mightie, I shall fill your stomack Master Peter: What two vpon one Sentlemen; Mistris
Miniver, much good doo't you Sir Adam.

SIR QUINTILIAN SHORTHOSE
Sir Vaughan, haue you din'd well Sir Vaughan?

SIR VAUGHAN
As good seere as would make any hungrie man (and a were in the vilest prison in the world) eate and
hee had anie stomacke: One word Sir Quintilian in hugger mugger; heere is a Sentleman of yours,
Master Peter Flash, is tesirous to haue his blew coate pul'd ouer his eares; and....

FLASH
No, Sir, my petition runs thus, that your whorshippe would thrust mee out of doores, and that I may
follow Sir Vaughan.

SIR VAUGHAN
I can tell you Master Flash, and you follow mee I goe verie fast, I thinke in my conscience, I am one of
the lightest knights in England.

FLASH
It's no matter Sir, the Flashes haue euer bin knowne to be quicke and light enough.

SIR QUINTILIAN SHORTHOSE
Sir Vaughan, he shal follow you, he shall dog you good Sir Vaughan.

Enter HORACE walking.

SIR VAUGHAN
Why then Peter Flash I will set my foure markes a yeare, and a blew coate vpon you.

FLASH
Godamercy to your worship, I hope you shall neuer repent for me.

SIR VAUGHAN
You beare the face of an honest man, for you blush passing well Peter, I will quench the flame out of your name, and you shall be christned Peter Salamander.

FLASH
The name's too good for me, I thanke your worship.

SIR VAUGHAN
Are you come Master Horace, you sent mee the Coppie of your letters countenance, and I did write and read it; your wittes truelie haue done verie valliantlie: tis a good inditements, you ha put in enough for her ha you not?

HORACE
According to my instructions.

SIR VAUGHAN
Tis passing well, I pray Master Horace walke a little beside your selfe, I will turne vpon you incontinent.

SIR QUINTILIAN SHORTHOSE
What Gentleman is this in the Mandilian, a soldyer?

SIR VAUGHAN
No, tho he has a very bad face for a souldier, yet he has as desperate a wit as euer any Scholler went to cuffes for; tis a Sentleman Poet, he has made rimes called Thalamimums, for M. Pride-groome, on vrd widdow.

SIR QUINTILIAN SHORTHOSE
Is this he? welcome Sir, your name? pray you walke not so statelie, but be acquainted with me boldlie; your name Sir?

HORACE
Quintus, Horacius, Flaccus.

SIR QUINTILIAN SHORTHOSE
Good Master Flappus welcome.

[He walkes vp and downe.

SIR VAUGHAN
Mistris Miniver, one vrde in your corner heere; I desire you to breake my armes heere, and read this Paper, you shall feele my mindes and affections in it, at full and at large.

MISTRIS MINIVER
Ile receiue no Loue libels perdy, but by word a mouth.

SIR VAUGHAN
By Sesu tis no libell, for heere is my hand to it.

MISTRIS MINIVER
Ile ha no hand in it Sir Vaughan, Ile not deale with you.

SIR VAUGHAN
Why then widdow, Ile tell you by word a mouth my deuices.

SIR QUINTILIAN SHORTHOSE
Your deuices come not neere my mouth Sir Vaughan perdy, I was vpon a time in the way to marriage,
but now I am turn'd a tother side, I ha sworne to leade a single and simple life.

SIR ADAM
She has answer'd you Sir Vaughan.

SIR VAUGHAN
Tis true, but at wrong weapons Sir Adam; will you be an Asse
Mistris Minivers?

MISTRIS MINIVER
If I be you shall not ride me.

SIR VAUGHAN
A simple life! by Sesu tis the life of a foole, a simple life!

SIR QUINTILIAN SHORTHOSE
How now Sir Vaughan?

SIR VAUGHAN
My braines has a little fine quawme come vnder it, and therefore Sir Adam, and Sir Quintilian, and
mistris Miniver caps God bo'y.

ALL
Good Sir Vaughan.

SIR VAUGHAN
Master Horace, your inuentions doe her no good in the Vniuersalities; yet heere is two shillings for your
wittes; nay by Sesu you shall take it if't were more: yonder bald Adams, is put my nose from his ioynt;
but Adam I will be euen to you: this is my cogitations, I will indite the Ladies & Miniuer caps to a dinner
of Plumbes, and I shall desire you M. Horace, to speake or raile; you can raile I hope in God a mighty.

HORACE
You meane to speake bitterlie.

SIR VAUGHAN

Right, to spitte bitterly vpon baldnes, or the thinnes of haire; you sall eate downe Plumbes to sweeten your mouth, and here is a good Ansell to defend you: Peter Salamander follow me.

FLASH
With hue and crie and you will Sir.

SIR VAUGHAN
Come M. Horace, I will goe pull out the Ladies.

HORACE
And Ile set out my wits, Baldnes the Theame?
My words shall flow hye in a siluer stream.

Exeunt.

Enter TUCCA brushing off the crumbes.

TUCCA
Wher's my most costly and sumptuous Shorthose?

SIR QUINTILIAN SHORTHOSE
Is the King risen from table Captaine Tucca?

TUCCA
How? risen? no my noble Quintilian, kings are greater men then we Knights and Caualliers, and therefore must eate more then lesser persons; Godamercy good Diues for these crummes: how now? Has not Frier Tucke din'd yet? he falles so hard to that Oyster-pye yonder.

SIR QUINTILIAN SHORTHOSE
Oyster-pye Captaine? ha, ha, he loues her, and I loue her and feare both shall goe without her.

TUCCA
Dost loue her, my finest and first part of the Mirrour of Knighthood? hange her she lookes like a bottle of ale, when the corke flyes out and the Ale fomes at mouth, shee lookes my good button-breech like the signe of Capricorne, or like Tiborne when it is couer'd with snow.

SIR QUINTILIAN SHORTHOSE
All's one for that, she has a vizard in a bagge, will make her looke like an Angell; I wod I had her, vpon condition, I gaue thee this chaine manlie Tucca.

TUCCA
I? saist thou so Friskin? I haue her ath hip for some causes, I can sound her, she'll come at my becke.

SIR QUINTILIAN SHORTHOSE
Wod I could sound her too Noble commaunder.

TUCCA

Thou shalt doo't; that Lady ath Lake is thine Sir Tristram, lend mee thy chaine, doe, lend it, Ile make her take it as a token, Ile lincke her vnto thee; and thou shalt weare her gloue in thy Worshipfull hatte like to a leather brooch; Nay and thou mistrusts thy coller, be tyed in't still.

SIR QUINTILIAN SHORTHOSE
Mistrust Captaine? no, heere tis, giue it her if she'll take it, or weare it thy selfe, if shee'll take mee, Ile watch him well enough too.

TUCCA
No more, Ile shoote away yonder Prickshaft, and then belabour her, and flye you after yonder Cucko: dost heere me my noble Gold-finch?—

SIR QUINTILIAN SHORTHOSE
No more.

TUCCA
How dost thou my smug Belimperia? how dost thou? hands off my little bald Derricke, hands off: harke hether Susanna, beware a these two wicked Elders, shall I speake well or ill of thee?

MISTRIS MINIVER
Nay, eene as you please Captaine, it shal be at your choise.

TUCCA
Why well said, my nimble Short-hose.

SIR QUINTILIAN SHORTHOSE
I heare her, I heare her.

TUCCA
Art angry father time? art angrie because I tooke mother-Winter aside? Ile holde my life thou art strucke with Cupids Birde-bolt, my little prickshaft, art? dost loue that mother Mumble-crust, dost thou? dost long for that whim-wham?

SIR ADAM
Wod I were as sure to lye with her, as to loue her.

TUCCA
Haue I found thee my learned Dunce, haue I found thee? If I might ha my wil, thou shouldst not put thy spoone into that bumble-broth (for indeede Ide taste her my selfe) no thou shouldst not; yet if her beautie blinde thee, she's thine, I can doo't, thou heardst her say eene now, it should bee at my choice.

SIR ADAM
She did so, worke the match and Ile bestow—

TUCCA
Not a silke point vpon mee, little Adam shee shall bee thy Eeue, for lesse then an Apple; but send, bee wise, send her some token, shee's greedie, shee shall take it, doe, send, thou shalt sticke in her (Prickeshaft) but send.

SIR ADAM
Heer's a purse of golde, thinke you that wil be accepted?

TUCCA
Goe to, it shall bee accepted, and twere but siluer, when that Flea-bitten Short-hose steppes hence: vanish too, and let mee alone with my Grannam in Gutter-Lane there, and this purse of golde doe, let me alone.

SIR QUINTILIAN SHORTHOSE
The King, gods Lord, I doe forget the King; Widdow, thinke on my wordes, I must be gone To waite his rising, Ile returne anone.

SIR ADAM
Stay Sir Quintilian, Ile be a waiter too.

SIR QUINTILIAN SHORTHOSE
Widdow wee'll trust that Captaine there with you.

Exeunt.

TUCCA
Now, now, mother Bunch how dost thou? what dost frowne Queene Gwyniuer? dost wrinckle? what made these paire of Shittle-cockes heere? what doe they fumble for? Ile ha none of these Kites fluttering about thy carkas, for thou shalt bee my West Indyes, and none but trim Tucca shall discouer thee.

MISTRIS MINIVER
Discouer me? discouer what thou canst of me.

TUCCA
What I can? thou knowst what I can discouer, but I will not lay thee open to the world.

MISTRIS MINIVER
Lay me open to the world?

TUCCA
No I will not my moldie decay'd Charing-crosse, I will not.

MISTRIS MINIVER
Hang thee patch-pannell, I am none a thy Charing-crosse: I scorne to be Crosse to such a scab as thou makst thy selfe.

TUCCA
No, tis thou makst me so, my Long Meg a Westminster, thou breedst a scab, thou—

MISTRIS MINIVER
I? dam thee filthie Captaine, dam thy selfe.

TUCCA

My little deuill a Dow-gate, Ile dam thee, (thou knowst my meaning) Ile dam thee vp; my wide mouth at Bishops-gate.

MISTRIS MINIVER

Wod I might once come to that damming.

TUCCA

Why thou shalt, my sweet dame Annis a cleere thou shalt, for Ile drowne my selfe in thee; I, for thy loue, Ile sinke, I, for thee.

MISTRIS MINIVER

So thou wilt I warrant, in thy abhominable sinnes; Lord,Lord, howe many filthy wordes hast thou to answere for.

TUCCA

Name one Madge-owlet, name one, Ile answer for none; my words shall be foorth comming at all times, & shall answer for them selues; my nimble Cat-a-mountaine: they shall Sislie Bum-trincket, for Ile giue thee none but Suger-candie wordes, I will not Pusse: goody Tripe-wife, I will not.

MISTRIS MINIVER

Why dost call mee such horrible vngodlie names then?

TUCCA

Ile name thee no more Mother Red-cap vpon paine of death, if thou wilt Grimalkin, Maggot-a-pye I will not.

MISTRIS MINIVER

Wod thou shouldst wel know, I am no Maggot, but a meere
Gentlewoman borne.

TUCCA

I know thou art a Gentle, and Ile nibble at thee, thou shalt be my Cap-a-maintenance, & Ile carrie my naked sword before thee, my reuerend Ladie Lettice-cap.

MISTRIS MINIVER

Thou shalt carry no naked swords before me to fright me, thou—

TUCCA

Go too, let not thy tongue play so hard at hot-cockles; for, Gammer Gurton, I meane to bee thy needle, I loue thee, I loue thee, because thy teeth stand like the Arches vnder London Bridge, for thou't not turne Satyre & bite thy husband; No, come my little Cub, doe not scorne mee because I goe in Stag, in Buffe, heer's veluet too; thou seest I am worth thus much in bare veluet.

MISTRIS MINIVER

I scorne thee not, not I.

TUCCA

I know thou dost not, thou shat see that I could march with two or three hundred linkes before me, looke here, what? I could shew golde too, if that would tempt thee, but I will not make my selfe a Gold-smithes stall I; I scorne to goe chain'd my Ladie ath Hospitall, I doe; yet I will and must bee chain'd to thee.

MISTRIS MINIVER

To mee? why Master Captaine, you know that I haue my choise of three or foure payre of Knights, and therefore haue small reason to flye out I know not how in a man of war.

TUCCA

A man a warre? come thou knowst not what a worshipfull focation tis to be a Captaines wife: three or four payre of Knights? why dost heare Ioane-a-bedlam, Ile enter into bond to be dub'd by what day thou wilt, when the next action is layde vpon me, thou shalt be Ladified.

MISTRIS MINIVER

You know I am offered that by halfe a dozen.

TUCCA

Thou shalt little Miniuer, thou shalt, Ile ha this frock turn'd into a foote-cloth; and thou shalt be carted, drawne I meane, Coacht, Coacht, thou shalt ryde Iigga-logge; a Hood shall flap vp and downe heere, and this shipskin-cap shall be put off.

MISTRIS MINIVER

Nay perdie, Ile put off my cap for no mans pleasure.

TUCCA

Wut thou be proude little Lucifer? well, thou shalt goe how thou wilt Maide-marian; come, busse thy little Anthony now, now, my cleane Cleopatria; so, so, goe thy waies Alexis secrets, th'ast a breath as sweet as the Rose, that growes by the Beare-garden, as sweete as the proud'st heade a Garlicke in England: come, wut march in, to the Gentle folkes?

MISTRIS MINIVER

Nay trulie Captaine you shall be my leader.

TUCCA

I say Mary Ambree, thou shalt march formost,
Because Ile marke how broad th'art in the heeles.

MISTRIS MINIVER

Perdie, I will be set ath last for this time.

TUCCA

Why then come, we'll walke arme in arme,
As tho we were leading one another to Newgate.

Enter BLUNt, CRISPINUS, and DEMETRIUS, with papers, laughing.

CRISPINUS
Mine's of a fashion, cut out quite from yours.

DEMETRIUS
Mine has the sharpest tooth, yonder he is.

BLUNT
Captaine Tucca.

All hold vp papers.

TUCCA
How now? I cannot stand to read supplications now.

CRISPINUS
They're bitter Epigrams compos'd on you
By Horace.

DEMETRIUS
And disperst amongst the gallants
In seuerall coppies, by Asinius Bubo.

TUCCA
By that liue Eele? read, Lege Legito, read thou lacke.

BLUNT
Tucca's growne monstrous, how? rich? that I feare,
He's to be seene for money euery where.

TUCCA
Why true, shall not I get in my debts, nay and the roague write no better I care not, farewell blacke lacke farewell.

CRISPINUS
But Captaine heer's a nettle.

TUCCA
Sting me, doe.

CRISPINUS
Tucca's exceeding tall and yet not hye,
He fights with skill, but does most vilye lye.

TUCCA
Right, for heere I lye now, open, open, to make my aduersarie come on; and then Sir, heere am I in's bosome: nay and this be the worst, I shal hug the poore honest face-maker, Ile loue the little Atheist, when he writes after my commendation, another whip? come yerke me.

DEMETRIUS
Tucca will bite, how? growne Satiricall,
No, he bites tables, for he feedes on all.

TUCCA
The whoreson clouen-foote deuill in mans apparell lyes,
There stood aboue forty dishes before me to day,
That I nere toucht, because they were empty.

MISTRIS MINIVER
I am witnes young Gentlemen to that.

TUCCA
Farewell stinckers, I smel thy meaning Screech-owle, I doe tho I stop my nose: and Sirra Poet, we'll haue
thee vntrust for this; come, mother Mum-pudding, come.

Exeunt.

SCENE II

Trumpets sound a florish, and then a sennate: Enter KING with CELESTINE, SIR WALTER TERRILL, SIR
QUINTILIAN, SIR ADAM, BLUNT and other Ladies and attendants: whilst the Trumpets sound the KING
takes his leaue of the Bride-groome, and SIR QUINTILIAN, and last of the Bride.

KING
My song of parting doth this burden beare;
A kisse the Ditty, and I set it heere.
Your lips are well in tune, strung with delight,
By this faire Bride remember soone at night:
Sir Walter.

TERRILL
My Leige Lord, we all attend,
The time and place.

KING
Till then my leaue commend.

They bring him to the doore:

Enter at another doore SIR VAUGHAN.

SIR VAUGHAN
Ladies, I am to put a verie easie suite vpon you all, and to desire you to fill your little pellies at a dinner
of plums behind noone; there be Suckets, and Marmilads, and Marchants, and other long white

plummes that faine would kisse your delicate and sweet lippes; I indite you all together, and you especially my Ladie Pride; what doe you saie for your selles? for I indite you all.

CELESTINE
I thanke you good Sir Vaughan, I will come.

SIR VAUGHAN
Say Sentlewomen will you stand to me too?

ALL
Wee'll sit with you sweet Sir Vaughan.

SIR VAUGHAN
God a mightie plesse your faces, and make your peauties
last, when wee are all dead and rotten:—you all will come.

1st LADY
All will come.

SIR VAUGHAN
Pray God that Horace bee in his right wittes to raile now.

Exit.

CRISPINUS
Come Ladie, you shall be my dauncing guest
To treade the maze of musicke with the rest.

DEMETRIUS
Ile lead you in.

DICACHE
A maze is like a doubt:
Tis easie to goe in, hard to get out.

BLUNT
We follow close behinde.

PHILOCALIA
That measure's best.
Now none markes vs, but we marke all the rest.

Exeunt.

Exeunt all sauing SIR QUINTILIAN, CELESTINE, and SIR WALTER TERRILL.

TERRILL
Father, and you my Bride; that name to day,

Wife, comes not till to morrow: but omitting
This enterchange of language; let vs thinke
Vpon the King and night, and call our spirits
To a true reckoning; first to Arme our wittes
With compleat steele of Iudgement, and our tongs,
With sound attillery of Phrases: then
Our Bodies must bee motions; moouing first
What we speake: afterwards, our very knees
Must humbly seeme to talke, and sute our speech;
For a true furnisht Cortyer hath such force,
Though his tonge faints, his very legs discourse.

SIR QUINTILIAN SHORTHOSE
Sonne Terrill, thou hast drawne his picture right,
For hee's noe full-made Courtier, nor well strung,
That hath not euery ioynt stucke with a tongue.
Daughter, if Ladies say, that is the Bride, that's she,
Gaze thou at none, for all will gaze at thee.

CELESTINE
Then, ô my father must I goe? O my husband
Shall I then goe? O my selfe, will I goe?

SIR QUINTILIAN SHORTHOSE
You must.

TERRILL
You shall.

CELESTINE
I will, but giue me leaue,
To say I may not, nor I ought not, say not
Still, I must goe, let me intreate I may not.

TERRILL
You must and shall, I made a deede of gift,
And gaue my oath vnto the King, I swore
By thy true constancy.

CELESTINE
Then keep that word
To sweare by, O let me be constant still.

TERRILL
What shall I cancell faith, and breake my oath?

CELESTINE
If breaking constancie, thou breakst them both.

TERRILL
Thy constancie no euill can pursue.

CELESTINE
I may be constant still, and yet not true.

TERRILL
As how?

CELESTINE
As thus, by violence detain'd,
They may be constant still, that are constrain'd.

TERRILL
Constrain'd? that word weighs heauy, yet my oath
Weighes downe that word; the kinges thoughts are at oddes,
They are not euen ballanst in his brest;
The King may play the man with me; nay more,
Kings may vsurpe; my wife's a woman; yet
Tis more then I know yet, that know not her,
If she should prooue mankinde, twere rare, fye, fye,
See how I loose my selfe, amongst my thoughts,
Thinking to finde my selfe; my oath, my oath.

SIR QUINTILIAN SHORTHOSE
I sweare another, let me see, by what,
By my long stocking, and my narrow skirtes,
Not made to sit vpon, she shall to Court.
I haue a tricke, a charme, that shall lay downe
The spirit of lust, and keep thee vndeflowred;
Thy husbands honor sau'd, and the hot King,
Shall haue enough too. Come, a tricke, a charme.

Exit.

CELESTINE
God keep thy honour safe, my bloud from harme.

TERRILL
Come, my sicke-minded Bride, Ile teach thee how,
To relish health a little: Taste this thought,
That when mine eyes seru'd loues commission,
Vpon thy beauties I did seise on them,
To a Kings vse; cure all thy griefe with this,
That his great seale was grauen vpon this ring,
And that I was but Steward to a King.

Exeunt.

ACT IV.

SCENE I. Banquet Hall in the House of Sir Vaughan

A banquet set out:

Enter SIR VAUGHAN, HORACE, ASINUS BUBO, LADY PETULA, DICACHE, PHILOCALIA, MISTRIS MINIVER and PETER FLASH.

SIR VAUGHAN
Ladies and Sentlemen, you are almost all welcome, to this sweet nuncions of Plums.

DICACHE
Almost all Sir Vaughan? why to which of vs are you so niggardly, that you cut her out but a peice of welcome.

SIR VAUGHAN
My interpretations is that almost all are welcome, because I indited a brace or two more that is not come, I am sorrie my Ladie Pride is not among you.

ASINIUS BUBO
Slid, he makes hounds of vs Ningle, a brace quoth a?

SIR VAUGHAN
Peter Salamanders draw out the pictures of all the ioynt stooles, & Ladies sit downe vpon their wodden faces.

FLASH
I warrant Sir, Ile giue euerie one of them a good stoole.

SIR VAUGHAN
Master Horace, Master Horace, when I pray to God, and desire in hipocritnes that bald Sir Adams were heer, then, then, then begin to make your railes at the pouertie and beggerly want of haire.

HORACE
Leaue it to my iudgement.

SIR VAUGHAN
M. Bubo sit there, you and I wil thinke vpon our ends at the Tables: M. Horace, put your learned bodie into the midst of these Ladies; so tis no matter to speake graces at nuncions, because we are all past grace since dinner.

ASINIUS BUBO

Mas I thanke my destinie I am not past grace, for by this hand full of Carrawaies, I could neuer abide to say grace.

DICACHE
Mistris Miniver, is not that innocent Gentleman a kinde of foole?

MISTRIS MINIVER
Why doe you aske Madam?

DICACHE
Nay for no harme, I aske because I thought you two had been of acquaintaine.

MISTRIS MINIVER
I thinke he's within an Inch of a foole.

DICACHE
Madam Philocalia, you sit next that spare Gentleman, wod you heard what Mistris Miniver saies of you.

PHILOCALIA
Why what saies she Madam Dicache.

DICACHE
Nay nothing, but wishes you were married to that small timber'd gallant.

PHILOCALIA
Your wish and mine are twinnes, I wish so too, for Then I should be sure to lead a merrie life.

ASINIUS BUBO
Yes faith Ladie, Ide make you laugh, my bolts now and then should be soone shot; by these comfits, weed let all slide.

PETULA
He takes the sweetest oathes that euer I heard a gallant of his pitch sweare; by these Comfits, & these Carrawaies, I warrant it does him good to sweare.

ASINIUS BUBO
Yes faith tis meate and drinke to me.
I am glad Ladie Petula (by this Apple) that they please you.

SIR VAUGHAN
Peter Salamanders wine, I beseech you Master Asinius Bubo, not to sweare so deeplie, for there comes no fruite of your oathes; heere Ladies, I put you all into one corners together, you shall all drinke of one cup.

ASINIUS BUBO
Peter I prethee fill me out too.

FLASH

Ide fling you out too and I might ha my will, a pox of all fooles.

SIR VAUGHAN
Mistris Minivers, pray bee lustie, wod Sir Adams Prickshaft stucke by you.

HORACE
Who, the balde Knight Sir Vaughan?

SIR VAUGHAN
The same M. Horace, he that has but a remnant or parcell of haire, his crowne is clipt and par'd away; me thinkes tis an excellent quallitie to bee balde; for and there stucke a nose and two nyes in his pate, he might weare two faces vnder one hood.

ASINIUS BUBO
As God saue me la, if I might ha my will, Ide rather be a balde Gentleman then a hairy; for I am sure the best and tallest Yeomen in England haue balde heads: me thinkes haire is a scuruie lowsie commodity.

HORACE
Bubo, heerein you blaze your ignorance.

SIR VAUGHAN
Pray stop and fill your mouthes, and giue M. Horace all your eares.

HORACE
For, if of all the bodies parts, the head
Be the most royall: if discourse, wit, Iudgement,
And all our vnderstanding faculties,
Sit there in their high Court of Parliament,
Enacting lawes to sway this humorous world:
This little Ile of Man: needes must that crowne,
Which stands vpon this supreame head, be faire,
And helde inualuable, and that crowne's the Haire:
The head that wants this honour stands awry,
Is bare in name and in authority.

SIR VAUGHAN
He meanes balde-pates Mistris Minivers.

HORACE
Haire, tis the roabe which curious nature weaues,
To hang vpon the head: and does adorne,
Our bodies in the first houre we are borne:
God does bestow that garment: when we dye,
That (like a soft and silken Canopie)
Is still spred ouer vs; In spight of death
Our hayre growes in our graue, and that alone
Lookes fresh, when all our other beauty's gone.
The excellence of Haire, in this shines cleere,

That the foure Elements take pride to weare
The fashion of it: when Fire most bright does burne,
The flames to golden lockes doe striue to turne;
When her lasciuious armes the Water hurles,
About the shoares wast, her sleeke head she curles:
And rorid cloudes being suckt into the Ayre,
When downe they melt, hangs like fine siluer hayre.
You see the Earth (whose head so oft is shorne)
Frighted to feele her lockes so rudely torne,
Stands with her haire an end, and (thus afraide)
Turnes euery haire to a greene naked blade.
Besides, when (strucke with griefe) we long to dye,
We spoile that most, which most does beautifie,
We rend this Head-tyre off. I thus conclude,
Cullors set cullors out; our eyes iudge right,
Of vice or vertue by their opposite:
So, if faire haire to beauty ad such grace,
Baldnes must needes be vgly, vile and base.

SIR VAUGHAN
True M. Horace, for a bald reason, is a reason that has no haires vpon't, a scuruy scalded reason.

MISTRIS MINIVER
By my truely I neuer thought you could ha pickt such strange things out of haire before.

ASINIUS BUBO
Nay my Ningle can tickle it, when hee comes too't.

MISTRIS MINIVER
Troth I shall neuer bee enameld of a bare-headed man for this, what shift so euer I make.

SIR VAUGHAN
Then Mistris Miniver Sir Adams Prickshaft must not hit you; Peter take vp all the cloathes at the table and the Plums.

Enter TUCCA and his BOY.

TUCCA
Saue thee my little worshipfull Harper; how doe yee my little cracknels? how doe ye?

SIR VAUGHAN
Welcome M. Tucca, sit and shoote into your belly some
Suger pellets.

TUCCA
No, Godamercy Cadwallader, how doe you Horace?

HORACE

Thankes good Captaine.

TUCCA
Wher's the Sering thou carriest about thee? O haue I found thee my scowring-sticke; what's my name Bubo?

ASINIUS BUBO
Wod I were hang'd if I can call you any names but Captaine and Tucca.

TUCCA
No Fye'st; my name's Hamlet reuenge: thou hast been at Parris garden hast not?

HORACE
Yes Captaine, I ha plaide Zulziman there.

SIR VAUGHAN
Then M. Horace you plaide the part of an honest man.

TUCCA
Death of Hercules, he could neuer play that part well in's life, no Fulkes you could not: thou call'st Demetrius Iorneyman Poet, but thou putst vp a Supplication to be a poore Iorneyman Player, and hadst beene still so, but that thou couldst not set a good face vpon't: thou hast forgot how thou amblest (in leather pilch) by a play-wagon, in the high way, and took'st mad Ieronimoes part, to get seruice among the Mimickes: and when the Stagerites banisht thee into the Ile of Dogs, thou turn'dst Bandog (villanous Guy) & euer since bitest therefore I aske if th'ast been at Parris-garden, because thou hast such a good mouth; thou baitst well, read, lege, saue thy selfe and read.

HORACE
Why Captaine these are Epigrams compos'd on you.

TUCCA
Goe not out Farding Candle, goe not out, for trusty Damboys now the deed is done, Ile pledge this Epigram in wine, Ile swallow it, I, yes.

SIR VAUGHAN
God blesse vs, will he be drunke with nittigrams now.

TUCCA
So, now arise sprite ath Buttry; no Herring-bone Ile not pull thee out, but arise deere Eccho rise, rise deuill or Ile coniure thee vp.

MISTRIS MINIVER
Good Master Tucca lets ha no coniuring heere.

SIR VAUGHAN
Vddes bloud you scald gouty Captaine, why come you to set encombrances heere betweene the Ladies.

TUCCA

Be not so tart my precious Metheglin, be not (my old whore a Babilon, sit fast.)

MISTRIS MINIVER
O Iesu if I know where abouts in London Babilon stands.

TUCCA
Feede and be fat my faire Calipolis, stir not my beauteous wriggle-tailes, Ile disease none of you, Ile take none of you vp, but onely this table-man, I must enter him into some filthy sincke point, I must.

HORACE
Captaine, you doe me wrong thus to disgrace me.

TUCCA
Thou thinkst thou maist be as sawcy with me as my Buffe Ierkin, to sit vpon me, dost?

HORACE
Dam me, if euer I traduc'd your name,
What imputation can you charge me with?

SIR VAUGHAN
Shlud, I, what cõputations can you lay to his sarge? answer, or by Sesu Ile canuas your coxcombe Tucky.

MISTRIS MINIVER
If they draw sweet hearts, let vs shift for our selues.

TUCCA
My noble swaggerer, I wil not fall out with thee, I cannot my mad Cumrade, finde in my heart to shed thy bloud.

SIR VAUGHAN
Cumrade? by Sesu call me Cumrade againe, and Ile Cumrade ye about the sinnes and shoulders; ownds, what come you to smell out heere? did you not dine and feede horribly well to day at dinner, but you come to munch heere, and giue vs winter-plummes? I pray depart, goe marse, marse, marse out a doores.

TUCCA
Adew Sir Eglamour, adew Lute-stringe, Curtin-rod, Goose-quill; heere, giue that full-nos'd Skinker, these rimes; & harke, Ile tagge my Codpeece point with thy legs, spout-pot Ile empty thee.

ASINIUS BUBO
Dost threaten mee? Gods lid Ile binde thee to the good forbearing.

SIR VAUGHAN
Will you amble Hobby-horse, will you trot and amble?

TUCCA
Raw Artichocke I shall sauce thee.

Exit.

MISTRIS MINIVER
I pray you Master Tucca, will you send me the fiue pound you borrowed on me; O you cannot heare now, but Ile make you heare me and feele me too in another place, to your shame I warrant you, thou shalt not conny-catch mee for fiue pounds; he tooke it vp Sir Vaughan in your name, hee swore you sent for it to Mum withall, twas fiue pound in gold, as white as my kercher.

SIR VAUGHAN
Ownds, fiue pound in my name to Mum about withall.

MISTRIS MINIVER
I, to Mum withall, but hee playes mum-budget with me.

SIR VAUGHAN
Peter Salamander, tye vp your great and your little sword, by Sesu Ile goe sing him while tis hot. Ile beate fiue pound out of his leather pilch: Master Horace, let your wittes inhabite in your right places; if I fall hansomely vpon the Widdow, I haue some cossens Garman at Court, shall beget you the reuersion of the Master of the Kings Reuels, or else be his Lord of Mis-rule nowe at Christmas: Come Ladyes, whoreson Stragling Captaine, Ile pound him.

Exeunt.

Enter HORACE and ASINIUS.

HORACE
How now? what ail'st thou, that thou look'st so pale.

ASINIUS BUBO
Nay nothing, but I am afraide the Welsh Knight has giuen me nothing but purging Comfits: this Captaine stickes pockily in my stomack; read this scroule, he saies they'r rimes, and bid me giue them you.

HORACE
Rimes? tis a challenge sent to you.

ASINIUS BUBO
To me?

HORACE
He saies heere you divulg'd my Epigrams.

ASINIUS BUBO
And for that dares he challenge me?

HORACE
You see he dares, but dare you answer him?

ASINIUS BUBO

I dare answer his challenge, by word of mouth, or by writing, but I scorne to meete him, I hope he and I are not Paralels.

HORACE
Deere Bubo, thou shalt answere him; our credites
Lye pawn'd vpon thy resolution,
Thy vallor must redeeme them; charge thy spirits,
To waite more close, and neere thee: if he kill thee,
Ile not suruiue; into one Lottery
We'll cast our fates; together liue and dye.

ASINIUS BUBO
Content, I owe God a death, and if he will make mee pay't against my will, Ile say tis hard dealing.

Exeunt.

SCENE II. A Street

Enter SIR ADAM, TUCCA, with two pistols by his sides, his boy laden with swords and bucklers.

TUCCA
Did Apolloes Freeze gowne watchman (boy, dost heare Turkie-cockes tayle, haue an eye behinde, least the enemie assault our Rere-ward) on proceede Father Adam; did that same tiranicall-tongu'd rag-a-muffin Horace, turne bald-pates out so naked?

SIR ADAM
He did, and whipt them so with nettles, that
The Widdow swore that a bare-headed man,
Should not man her: the Ladie Petula
Was there, heard all, and tolde me this.

TUCCA
Goe too. Thy golde was accepted, it was, and she shall bring thee into her Paradice, she shall small Adam, she shall.

SIR ADAM
But how? but how Capten?

TUCCA
Thus, goe, couer a table with sweet meates, let all the Gentlewomen, and that same Pasquils-mad-cap (mother Bee there) nibble, bid them bite: they will come to gobble downe Plummes; then take vp that paire of Basket hiltes, with my commission, I meane Crispinus and Fannius; charge one of them to take vp the Bucklers, against that hayre-monger Horace, and haue a bout or two, in defence of balde-pates: let them cracke euerie crowne that has haire on't: goe, let them lift vp baldenes to the skie, and thou shalt see, twill turne Miniuers heart quite against the haire.

SIR ADAM
Excellent, why then M. Tucca—

TUCCA
Nay, whir, nymble Prickshaft; whir, away, I goe vpon life and death, away, flie Scanderbag flie.

Exit.

Enter ASINIUS BUBO, and HORACE aloofe.

BOY
Arme Captaine, arme, arme, arme, the foe is come downe.

TUCCA offers to shoote.

ASINIUS BUBO
Hold Capten Tucca holde, I am Bubo, & come to answer any thing you can lay to my charge.

TUCCA
What, dost summon a parlie my little Drumsticke? tis too late; thou seest my red flag is hung out, Ile fill thy guts with thine owne carrion carcas, and then eate them vp in steed of Sawsages.

ASINIUS BUBO
Vse me how you will; I am resolute, for I ha made my Will.

TUCCA
Wilt fight Turke-a-ten-pence? wilt fight then?

ASINIUS BUBO
Thou shalt finde Ile fight in a Godly quarrell, if I be once fir'd.

TUCCA
Thou shalt not want fire, Ile ha thee burnt when thou wilt, my colde Cornelius: but come: Respice funem; looke, thou seest; open thy selfe my little Cutlers Shoppe, I challenge thee thou slender Gentleman, at foure sundrie weapons.

ASINIUS BUBO
Thy challenge was but at one, and Ile answere but one.

BOY
Thou shalt answer two, for thou shalt answer me and my Capten.

TUCCA
Well said Cockrell out-crowe him: art hardy noble Huon? art Magnanimious? licke-trencher; looke, search least some lye in ambush; for this man at Armes has paper in's bellie, or some friend in a corner, or else hee durst not bee so cranke.

BOY

Capten, Capten, Horace stands sneaking heere.

TUCCA
I smelt the foule-fisted Morter-treader, come my most damnable fastidious rascall, I haue a suite to both
of you.

ASINIUS BUBO
O holde, most pittifull Captaine holde.

HORACE
Holde Capten, tis knowne that Horace is valliant, & a man of the sword.

TUCCA
A Gentleman or an honest Cittizen, shall not Sit in your pennie-bench Theaters, with his Squirrell by his
side cracking nuttes; nor sneake into a Tauerne with his Mermaid; but he shall be Satyr'd, and Epigram'd
vpon, and his humour must run vpo'th Stage: you'll ha Euery Gentleman in's humour, and Euery
Gentleman out on's humour: wee that are heades of Legions and Bandes, and feare none but these
same shoulder-clappers, shall feare you, you Serpentine rascall.

HORACE
Honour'd Capten.

TUCCA
Art not famous enough yet, my mad Horastratus, for killing a Player, but thou must eate men aliue? thy
friends? Sirra wilde-man, thy Patrons? thou Anthropophagite, thy Mecænasses?

HORACE
Captaine, I'm sorry that you lay this wrong
So close vnto your heart: deare Captaine thinke
I writ out of hot bloud, which (now) being colde,
I could be pleas'd (to please you) to quaffe downe,
The poyson'd Inke, in which I dipt your name.

TUCCA
Saist thou so, my Palinodicall rimester?

HORACE
Hence forth Ile rather breath out Solœcismes
(To doe which Ide as soone speake blasphemie)
Than with my tongue or pen to wound your worth,
Beleeue it noble Capten; it to me
Shall be a Crowne, to crowne your actes with praize,
Out of your hate, your loue Ile stronglie raize.

TUCCA
I know now th'ast a number of these Quiddits to binde men to'th peace: tis thy fashion to flirt Inke in
euerie mans face; and then to craule into his bosome, and damne thy selfe to wip't off agen: yet to giue
out abroad, that hee was glad to come to composition with thee: I know Monsieur Machiauell tis one a

thy rules; My long-heel'd Troglodite, I could make thine eares burne now, by dropping into them, all those hot oathes, to which, thy selfe gau'st voluntarie fire, (whē thou wast the man in the Moone) that thou wouldst neuer squib out any new Salt-peter Iestes against honest Tucca, nor those Maligo-tasters, his Poetasters; I could Cinocephalus, but I will not, yet thou knowst thou hast broke those oathes in print, my excellent infernall.

HORACE
Capten.

TUCCA
Nay I smell what breath is to come from thee, thy answer is, that there's no faith to be helde with Heritickes & Infidels, and therfore thou swear'st anie thing: but come, lend mee thy hand, thou and I hence forth will bee Alexander and Lodwicke, the Gemini: sworne brothers, thou shalt be Perithous and Tucca Theseus; but Ile leaue thee i'th lurch, when thou mak'st thy voiage into hell:
till then, Thine-assuredly.

HORACE
With all my soule deare Capten.

TUCCA
Thou'lt shoote thy quilles at mee, when my terrible backe's turn'd for all this, wilt not Porcupine? and bring me & my Heliconistes into thy Dialogues to make vs talke madlie wut not Lucian?

HORACE
Capten, if I doe—

TUCCA
Nay and thou dost, hornes of Lucifer, the Parcell-Poets shall Sue thy wrangling Muse, in the Court of Pernassus, and neuer leaue hunting her, till she pleade in Forma Pauperis: but I hope th'ast more grace: come: friendes, clap handes, tis a bargaine; amiable Bubo, thy fist must walke too: so, I loue thee, now I see th'art a little Hercules, and wilt fight; Ile Sticke thee now in my companie like a sprig of Rosemary.

Enter SIR REES ap VAUGHAN and PETER FLASH.

FLASH
Draw Sir Rees he's yonder, shall I vpon him?

SIR VAUGHAN
Vpon him? goe too, goe too Peter Salamander; holde, in Gods name holde; I will kill him to his face, because I meane he shall answer for it; being an eye-witnes; one vrde Capten Tucky.

TUCCA
Ile giue thee ten thousand words and thou wilt, my little Thomas Thomasius.

SIR VAUGHAN
By Sesu, tis best you giue good vrdes too, least I beate out your tongue, and make your vrde nere to bee taken more; doe you heare, fiue pounds, fiue pounds Tucky.

TUCCA

Thou shalt ha fiue, and fiue, and fiue, and thou wantst money my Iob.

SIR VAUGHAN

Leaue your fetches and your fegaries, you tough leather-Ierkins; leaue your quandaries, and trickes, and draw vpon me y' are best: you conny-catch Widdow Miniuer-caps for fiue pounds, and say tis for me to cry Mum, and make mee run vp and downe in dishonors, and discredites; is 't not true, you winke-a-pipes rascall? is not true?

TUCCA

Right, true, guilty, I remember't now; for when I spake a good word to the Widdow for thee my young Sampson—

SIR VAUGHAN

For fiue pounds you cheating scab, for 5. pounds, not for me.

TUCCA

For thee ô Cæsar, for thee I tooke vp fiue pounds in golde, that lay in her lap, & said Ide giue it thee as a token from her: I did it but to smell out how she stood affected to thee, to feele her; I, and I know what she said, I know how I carried away the golde.

SIR VAUGHAN

By Sesu, I ha not the mercy to fall vpon him now: M. Tucky, did widdow Miniuers part quietly from her golde, because you lyed, and said it was for me?

TUCCA

Quietly, in peace, without grumbling; made no noise, I know how I tempted her in thy behalfe; my little Trangdo.

SIR VAUGHAN

Capten Tucky, I will pay back her 5. £. (vnles you be damn'd in lyes) & hold you, I pray you pocket vp this; by the crosse a this sword & dagger, Capten you shall take it.

TUCCA

Dost sweare by daggers? nay then Ile put vp more at thy hands then this.

FLASH

Is the fray done sir?

SIR VAUGHAN

Done Peter, put vp your smeeter.

TUCCA

Come hether, my soure-fac'd Poet; fling away that beard-brush Bubo, casheere him and harke: Knight attend: So, that raw-head and bloudy-bones Sir Adam, has fee'd another brat (of those nine common wenches) to defend baldnes and to raile against haire: he'll haue a fling at thee, my noble Cock-Sparrow.

SIR VAUGHAN

At mee? will hee fling the cudgels of his witte at mee?

TUCCA
And at thy button-cap too; but come, Ile be your leader, you shall stand, heare all, & not be seene; cast off that blew coate, away with that flawne, and follow, come.

Exit.

HORACE
Bubo, we follow Captaine.

SIR VAUGHAN
Peter, leaue comming behinde me, I pray any longer, for you and I must part Peter.

FLASH
Sounds Sir, I hope you will not serue me so, to turne me away in this case.

SIR VAUGHAN
Turne you into a fooles coate; I meane I will go solus, or in solitaries alone; ounds y-are best giue better words, or Ile turne you away indeed; where is Capten Tucky? come Horace; get you home Peter.

FLASH
Ile home to your cost, and I can get into the Wine-Seller.

Exit.

HORACE
Remember where to meete mee.

ASINIUS BUBO
Yes Ile meete; Tucca should ha found I dare meete.

Exit.

HORACE
Dare defend baldnes, which our conquering Muse
Has beaten downe so flat? Well, we will goe,
And see what weapons theyr weake wittes doe bring;
If sharpe, we'll spred a large and nobler wing;
Tucca, heere lyes thy Peace: warre roares agen;
My Swoord shall neuer cutte thee, but my pen.

Exit.

SCENE III. Sir Adam's Garden

Enter SIR ADAM, CRISPINUS, FANNIUS, BLUNT, MISTRESS MINIUER, PETULA, PHILOCALIA and DICACE.

LADIES
Thankes good Sir Adam.

SIR ADAM
Welcome red-cheekt Ladies,
And welcome comely Widdow; Gentlemen,
Now that our sorry banquet is put by,
From stealing more sweet kisses from your lips
Walke in my garden: Ladyes let your eyes
Shed life into these flowers by their bright beames,
Sit, Sit, heere's a large bower, heere all may heare,
Now good Crispinus let your praize begin
There, where it left off Baldnes.

CRISPINUS
I shall winne
No praise, by praising that, which to depraue,
All tongues are readie, and which none would haue.

BLUNT
To prooue that best, by strong and armed reason,
Whose part reason feares to take, cannot but prooue,
Your wit's fine temper, and from these win loue.

MISTRIS MINIVER
I promise you has almost conuerted me, I pray bring forward your bald reasons M. Poet.

CRISPINUS
Mistris you giue my Reasons proper names,
For Arguments (like Children) should be like,
The subiect that begets them; I must striue
To crowne Bald heades, therefore must baldlie thriue;
But be it as it can: To what before,
Went arm'd at table, this force bring I more,
If a Bare head (being like a dead-mans scull)
Should beare vp no praise els but this, it sets
Our end before our eyes; should I dispaire,
From giuing Baldnes higher place then haire?

MISTRIS MINIVER
Nay perdie, haire has the higher place.

CRISPINUS
The goodliest & most glorious strange-built wonder,
Which that great Architect hath made, is heauen;
For there he keepes his Court, It is his Kingdome,

That's his best Master-piece; yet tis the roofe,
And Seeling of the world: that may be cal'd
The head or crowne of Earth, and yet that's balde,
All creatures in it balde; the louely Sunne,
Has a face sleeke as golde; the full-cheekt Moone,
As bright and smooth as siluer: nothing there
Weares dangling lockes, but sometime blazing Starres,
Whose flaming curles, set realmes on fire with warres.
Descend more low; looke through mans fiue-folde sence,
Of all, the Eye, beares greatest eminence;
And yet that's balde, the haires that like a lace,
Are sticht vnto the liddes, borrow those formes,
Like Pent-houses to saue the eyes from stormes.

SIR ADAM
Right, well said.

CRISPINUS
A head and face ore-growne with Shaggie drosse,
O, tis an Orient pearle hid all in Mosse,
But when the head's all naked and vncrown'd,
It is the worlds Globe, euen, smooth and round;
Baldnes is natures But, at which our life,
Shootes her last Arrow: what man euer lead
His age out with a staffe, but had a head
Bare and vncouer'd? hee whose yeares doe rise,
To their full height, yet not balde, is not wise.
The Head is Wisedomes house, Haire but the thatch,
Haire? It's the basest stubble; in scorne of it,
This Prouerbe sprung, he has more haire then wit:
Marke you not in derision how we call,
A head growne thicke with haire, Bush-naturall?

MISTRIS MINIVER
By your leaue (Master Poet) but that Bush-naturall, is one a the trimmest, and most intanglingst beautie
in a woman.

CRISPINUS
Right, but beleeue this (pardon me most faire)
You would haue much more wit, had you lesse haire:
I could more wearie you to tell the proofes,
(As they passe by) which fight on Baldnes side,
Then were you taskt to number on a head,
The haires: I know not how your thoughts are lead,
On this strong Tower shall my opinion rest,
Heades thicke of haire are goode, but balde the best.

Whilst this Paradox is in speaking, TUCCA Enters with SIR VAUGHAN at one doore, and secretly placeth him: then Exit and brings in HORACE muffled, placing him: TUCCA sits among them.

TUCCA
Th'art within a haire of it, my sweete Wit whether wilt thou? my delicate Poeticall Furie, th' ast hit it to a haire.

SIR VAUGHAN steps out.

SIR VAUGHAN
By your fauour Master Tucky, his balde reasons are wide aboue two hayres, I besees you pardon mee Ladies, that I thrust in so malepartly among you, for I did but mych heere, and see how this cruell Poet did handle bald heades.

SIR ADAM
He gaue them but their due Sir Vaughan; Widdow did he not?

MISTRIS MINIVER
By my faith he made more of a balde head, than euer I shall be able: he gaue them their due truely.

SIR VAUGHAN
Nay vds bloud, their due is to bee a the right haire as I am, and that was not in his fingers to giue, but in God a Mighties: Well, I will hyre that humorous and fantasticall Poet Master Horace, to breake your balde pate Sir Adam.
Breake my balde pate?

TUCCA
Dost heare my worshipfull block-head?

SIR VAUGHAN
Patience Captaine Tucky, let me absolue him; I meane he shal pricke, pricke your head or sconce a little with his goose-quils, for he shal make another Thalimum, or crosse-stickes, or some Polinoddyes, with a fewe Nappy-grams in them, that shall lift vp haire, and set it an end, with his learned and harty commendations.

HORACE
This is excellent, all will come out now.
That same Horace me thinkes has the most vngodly face, by my Fan; it lookes for all the world, like a rotten russet Apple, when tis bruiz'd: Its better then a spoonefull of Sinamon water next my heart, for me to heare him speake; hee soundes it so i' th nose, and talkes and randes for all the world, like the poore fellow vnder Ludgate: oh fye vpon him.

MISTRIS MINIVER
By my troth sweet Ladies, it's Cake and pudding to me, to see his face make faces, when hee reades his Songs and Sonnets.

HORACE
Ile face some of you for this, when you shall not budge.

TUCCA
Its the stinckingst dung-farmer—foh vpon him.

SIR VAUGHAN
Foh? oundes you make him vrse than olde herring: foh? By Sesu I thinke he's as tidy, and as tall a Poet as euer drew out a long verse.

TUCCA
The best verse that euer I knew him hacke out, was his white necke-verse: noble Ap Rees thou wouldst scorne to laye thy lippes to his commendations, and thou smeldst him out as I doe, hee calles thee the burning Knight of the Salamander.

SIR VAUGHAN
Right, Peter is my Salamander; what of him? But Peter is neuer burnt: howe now? so, goe too now.

TUCCA
And sayes because thou Clipst the Kinges English.

SIR VAUGHAN
Oundes mee? that's treason: clip? horrible treasons,
Sesu holde my handes; clip? he baites mouse-trappes for my life.

TUCCA
Right little Twinckler, right: hee sayes because thou speak'st no better, thou canst not keepe a good tongue in thy head.

SIR VAUGHAN
By God tis the best tongue, I can buy for loue or money.

TUCCA
He shootes at thee too Adam Bell, and his arrowes stickes heere; he calles thee bald-pate.

SIR VAUGHAN
Oundes make him prooue these intollerabilities.

TUCCA
And askes who shall carry the vineger-bottle? & then he rimes too't, and sayes Prickshaft: nay Miniuer hee cromples thy Cap too; and—

CRISPINUS
Come Tucca, come, no more; the man's wel knowne, thou needst not
paint him, whom does he not wrong?

TUCCA
Mary himselfe, the vglie Pope Boniface, pardons himselfe, and therefore my iudgement is, that presently he bee had from hence to his place of execution, and there bee Stab'd, Stab'd, Stab'd.

He stabs at him.

HORACE
Oh gentlemen, I am slaine, oh slaue art hyr'd to murder me, to murder me, to murder me?

LADIES
Oh God!

SIR VAUGHAN
Ounds Capten, you haue put all Poetrie to the dint of sword, blow winde about him: Ladies for our Lordes sake you that haue smocks, teare off peeces, to shoote through his oundes: Is he dead and buried? is he? pull his nose, pinch, rub, rub, rub, rub.

TUCCA
If he be not dead, looke heere; I ha the Stab and pippin for him: if I had kil'd him, I could ha pleas'd the great foole with an Apple.

CRISPINUS
How now? be well good Horace, heer's no wound;
Y'are slaine by your owne feares; how dost thou man?
Come, put thy heart into his place againe;
Thy out-side's neither peir'st, nor In-side slaine.

SIR VAUGHAN
I am glad M. Horace, to see you walking.

HORACE
Gentlemen, I am blacke and blewe the breadth of a groate.

TUCCA
Breadth of a groate? there's a teston, hide thy infirmities, my scuruy Lazarus; doe, hide it, least it prooue a scab in time: hang thee desperation, hang thee, thou knowst I cannot be sharpe set against thee: looke, feele (my light-vptailes all) feele my weapon.

MISTRIS MINIVER
O most pittifull as blunt as my great thumbe.

SIR VAUGHAN
By Sesu, as blunt as a Welsh bag-pudding.

TUCCA
As blunt as the top of Poules; tis not like thy Aloe, Cicatrine tongue, bitter: no, tis no stabber, but like thy goodly and glorious nose, blunt, blunt, blunt: dost roare bulchin? dost roare? th' ast a good rounciuall voice to cry Lanthorne & Candlelight.

SIR VAUGHAN

Two vrds Horace about your eares: how chance it passes, that you bid God boygh to an honest trade of building Symneys, and laying downe Brickes, for a worse handicraftnes, to make nothing but railes; your Muse leanes vpon nothing but filthy rotten railes, such as stand on Poules head, how chance?

HORACE
Sir Vaughan.

SIR VAUGHAN
You lye sir varlet sir villaine, I am sir Salamanders, ounds, is my man Master Peter Salamanders face as vrse as mine? Sentlemen, all and Ladies, and you say once or twice Amen, I will lap this little Silde, this Booby in his blankets agen.

OMNES
Agree'd, agree'd.

TUCCA
A blanket, these crackt Venice glasses shall fill him out, they shall tosse him, holde fast wag-tailes: so, come, in, take this bandy with the racket of patience, why when? dost stampe mad Tamberlaine, dost stampe? thou thinkst th'ast Morter vnder thy feete, dost?

LADIES
Come, a bandy ho.

HORACE
O holde most sacred beauties.

SIR VAUGHAN
Hold, silence, the puppet-teacher speakes.

HORACE
Sir Vaughan, noble Capten, Gentlemen,
Crispinus, deare Demetrius ô redeeme me,
Out of this infamous— by God by Iesu—

CRISPINUS
Nay, sweare not so good Horace, now these Ladies,
Are made your executioners: prepare,
To suffer like a gallant, not a coward;
Ile trie t' vnloose, their hands, impossible.
Nay, womens vengeance are implacable.

HORACE
Why, would you make me thus the ball of scorne?

TUCCA
Ile tell thee why, because th' ast entred Actions of assault and battery, against a companie of honourable and worshipfull Fathers of the law: you wrangling rascall, law is one of the pillers ath land, and if thou beest bound too't (as I hope thou shalt bee) thou't prooue a skip-Jacke, thou't be whipt. Ile

tell thee why, because thy sputtering chappes yelpe, that Arrogance, and Impudence, and Ignoraunce, are the essentiall parts of a Courtier.

SIR VAUGHAN
You remember Horace, they will puncke, and pincke, and pumpe you, and they catch you by the coxcombe: on I pray, one lash, a little more.

TUCCA
Ile tell thee why, because thou cryest ptrooh at worshipfull Cittizens, and cal'st them Flat-caps, Cuckolds, and banckrupts, and modest and vertuous wiues punckes & cockatrices. Ile tell thee why, because th'ast arraigned two Poets against all lawe and conscience; and not content with that, hast turn'd them amongst a company of horrible blacke Fryers.

SIR VAUGHAN
The same hand still, it is your owne another day, M. Horace, admonitions is good meate.

TUCCA
Thou art the true arraign'd Poet, and shouldst haue been hang'd, but for one of these part-takers, these charitable Copperlac'd Christians, that fetcht thee out of Purgatory, (Players I meane) Theaterians pouch-mouth, Stage-walkers; for this Poet, for this, thou must lye with these foure wenches, in that blancket, for this—

HORACE
What could I doe, out of a iust reuenge,
But bring them to the Stage? they enuy me
because I holde more worthy company.

DEMETRIUS
Good Horace, no; my cheekes doe blush for thine,
As often as thou speakst so, where one true
And nobly-vertuous spirit, for thy best part
Loues thee, I wish one ten, euen from my heart.
I make account I put vp as deepe share
In any good mans loue, which thy worth earnes,
As thou thy selfe; we enuy not to see,
Thy friends with Bayes to crowne thy Poesie.
No, heere the gall lyes, we that know what stuffe
Thy verie heart is made of; know the stalke
On which thy learning growes, and can giue life
To thy (once dying) basenes; yet must we
Dance Antickes on your Paper.

HORACE
Fannius.

CRISPINUS
This makes vs angry, but not enuious,
No, were thy warpt soule, put in a new molde,

Ide weare thee as a Iewell set in golde.

SIR VAUGHAN
And Iewels Master Horace, must be hang'd you know.

TUCCA
Good Pagans, well said, they haue sowed vp that broken seame-rent lye of thine, that Demetrius is out at Elbowes, and Crispinus is falne out with Sattin heere, they haue; but bloate-herring dost heare?

HORACE
Yes honour'd Captaine, I haue eares at will.

TUCCA
Ist not better be out at Elbowes, then to bee a bond-slaue, and to goe all in Parchment as thou dost?

HORACE
Parchment Captaine? tis Perpetuana I assure you.

TUCCA
My Perpetuall pantaloone true, but tis waxt ouer; th'art made out of Wax; thou must answere for this one day; thy Muse is a hagler, and weares cloathes vpon best-be-trust: th'art great in some bodies books for this, thou knowst where; thou wouldst bee out at Elbowes, and out at heeles too, but that thou layest about thee with a Bill for this, a Bill—

HORACE
I confesse Capten, I followed this suite hard.

TUCCA
I know thou didst, and therefore whilst we haue Hiren heere,
speake my little dish-washers, a verdit Pisse-kitchins.

OMNES
Blancket.

SIR VAUGHAN
Holde I pray, holde, by Sesu I haue put vpon my heade, a fine deuice, to make you laugh, tis not your fooles Cap Master Horace, which you couer'd your Poetasters in, but a fine tricke, ha, ha, is iumbling in my braine.

TUCCA
Ile beate out thy braines, my whorson hansome dwarfe, but ile haue it out of thee.

OMNES
What is it good Sir Vaughan?

SIR VAUGHAN
To conclude, tis after this manners, because Ma. Horace is ambition, and does conspire to bee more hye and tall, as God a mightie made him, wee'll carry his terrible person to Court, and there before his

Masestie Dub, or what you call it, dip his Muse in some licour, and christen him, or dye him, into collours of a Poet.

OMNES
Excellent.

TUCCA
Super Super-excellent Reuellers goe, proceede you Masters of Arte in kissing these wenches, and in daunces, bring you the quiuering Bride to Court, in a Maske, come Crumboll, thou shalt Mum with vs; come, dogge mee skneakes-bill.

HORACE
O thou my Muse!

SIR VAUGHAN
Call vpon God a mighty, and no Muses, your Muse I warrant is otherwise occupied, there is no dealing with your Muse now, therefore I pray marse, marse, marse, oundes your Moose?

Exeunt.

CRISPINUS
We shal haue sport to see them; come bright beauties,
The Sunne stoops low, and whispers in our eares,
To hasten on our Maske, let's crowne this night,
With choise composed wreathes of sweet delight.

  Exeunt.

ACT V

SCENE I. Hall in the House of Sir Quintilian

Enter TERRILL and CELESTINE sadly, SIR QUINTILIAN stirring and mingling a cup of wine.

TERRILL
O Night, that Dyes the Firmament in blacke,
And like a cloth of cloudes doth stretch thy limbes;
Vpon the windy Tenters of the Ayre:
O thou that hang'st vpon the backe of Day,
Like a long mourning gowne: thou that art made
Without an eye, because thou shouldst not see
A Louers Reuels: nor participate
The Bride-groomes heauen; ô heauen, to me a hell:
I haue a hell in heauen, a blessed cursse;
All other Brides-groomes long for Night, and taxe
The Day of lazie slouth; call Time a Cripple,

And say the houres limpe after him: but I
Wish Night for euer banisht from the skie,
Or that the Day would neuer sleepe: or Time,
Were in a swound; and all his little Houres,
Could neuer lift him vp with their poore powers.

Enter CELESTINE.

But backward runnes the course of my delight;
The day hath turn'd his backe, and it is night;
This night will make vs odde; day made vs eeuen,
All else are damb'd in hel, but I in heauen.

CELESTINE
Let loose thy oath, so shall we still be eeuen.

TERRILL
Then am I damb'd in hell, and not in heauen.

CELESTINE
Must I then goe? tis easie to say no,
Must is the King himselfe, and I must goe;
Shall I then goe? that word is thine; I shall,
Is thy commaund: I goe because I shall;
Will I then goe? I aske my selfe; ô ill,
King, saies I must; you, I shall; I, I will.

TERRILL
Had I not sworne.

CELESTINE
Why didst thou sweare?

TERRILL
The King
Sat heauvy on my resolution,
Till (out of breath) it panted out an oath.

CELESTINE
An oath? why, what's an oath? tis but the smoake,
Of flame & bloud; the blister of the spirit,
Which rizeth from the Steame of rage, the bubble
That shootes vp to the tongue, and scaldes the voice,
(For oathes are burning words) thou swor'st but one,
Tis frozen long agoe: if one be numbred,
What Countrimen are they? where doe they dwell,
That speake naught else but oathes?

TERRILL
They're men of hell.
An oath? why tis the trafficke of the soule,
Tis law within a man; the seale of faith,
The bond of euery conscience; vnto whom,
We set our thoughts like hands: yea, such a one
I swore, and to the King: A King containes
A thousand thousand; when I swore to him,
I swore to them; the very haires that guard
His head, will rise vp like sharpe witnesses
Against my faith and loyalty: his eye
Would straight condemne me: argue oathes no more,
My oath is high, for to the King I swore.

Enter SIR QUINTILIAN with the cup.

CELESTINE
Must I betray my Chastity? So long
Cleane from the treason of rebelling lust;
O husband! O my Father! if poore I,
Must not liue chast, then let me chastly dye.

SIR QUINTILIAN
I, heer's a charme shall keep thee chaste, come, come,
Olde Time hath left vs but an houre to play
Our parts; begin the Sceane, who shall speake first?
Oh, I, I play the King, and Kings speake first;
Daughter stand thou heere, thou Sonne Terrill there,
O thou standst well, thou lean'st against a poast,
(For thou't be posted off I warrant thee:)
The King will hang a horne about thy necke,
And make a poast of thee; you stand well both,
We neede no Prologue, the King entring first,
He's a most gracious Prologue: mary then
For the Catastrophe, or Epilogue,
Ther's one in cloth of Siluer, which no doubt,
Will please the hearers well, when he steps out;
His mouth is fil'd with words: see where he stands;
He'll make them clap their eyes besides their hands.
But to my part; suppose who enters now,
A King, whose eyes are set in Siluer; one
That blusheth golde, speakes Musicke, dancing walkes,
Now gathers neerer takes thee by the hand,
When straight thou thinkst, the very Orbe of heauen,
Mooues round about thy fingers, then he speakes,
Thus—thus—I know not how.

CELESTINE

Nor I to answer him.

SIR QUINTILIAN SHORTHOSE
No girle? knowst thou not how to answer him?
Why then the field is lost, and he rides home,
Like a great conquerour; not answer him?
Out of thy part already? foylde the Sceane?
Disranckt the lynes? disarm'd the action?

TERRILL
Yes yes, true chastity is tongu'd so weake,
Tis ouer-come ere it know how to speake.

SIR QUINTILIAN SHORTHOSE
Come, come, thou happy close of euery wrong,
Tis thou that canst dissolue the hardest doubt;
Tis time for thee to speake, we are all out.
Daughter, and you the man whom I call Sonne,
I must confesse I made a deede of gift;
To heauen and you, and gaue my childe to both:
When on my blessing I did charme her soule,
In the white circle of true Chastity,
Still to run true, till death: now Sir if not,
She forfeyts my rich blessing, and is Fin'd
With an eternall cursse; then I tell you,
She shall dye now, now whilst her soule is true.

TERRILL
Dye?

CELESTINE
I, I am deaths eccho.

SIR QUINTILIAN SHORTHOSE
O my Sonne,
I am her Father; euery teare I shed,
Is threescore ten yeere olde; I weepe and smile
Two kinde of teares: I weepe that she must dye,
I smile that she must dye a Virgin: thus
We ioyfull men mocke teares, and teares mocke vs.

TERRILL
What speakes that cup?

SIR QUINTILIAN SHORTHOSE
White wine and poison.

TERRILL

Oh:
That very name of poison, poisons me;
Thou Winter of a man, thou walking graue,
Whose life is like a dying Taper: how
Canst thou define a Louers labouring thoughts?
What Sent hast thou but death? what taste but earth?
The breath that purles from thee, is like the Steame
Of a new-open'd vault: I know thy drift,
Because thou art trauelling to the land of Graues,
Thou couetst company, and hether bringst,
A health of poison to pledge death: a poison
For this sweete spring; this Element is mine,
This is the Ayre I breath; corrupt it not;
This heauen is mine, I bought it with my soule,
Of him that selles a heauen, to buy a soule.

SIR QUINTILIAN SHORTHOSE
Well, let her goe; she's thine thou cal'st her thine,
Thy Element, the Ayre thou breath'st; thou knowst
The Ayre thou breath'st is common, make her so:
Perhaps thou't say; none but the King shall weare
Thy night-gowne, she that laps thee warme with loue;
And that Kings are not common: Then to shew,
By consequence he cannot make her so,
Indeede she may promoote her shame and thine,
And with your shames, speake a good word for mine:
The King shining so cleare, and we so dim,
Our darke disgraces will be seene through him.
Imagine her the cup of thy moist life,
What man would pledge a King in his owne wife?

TERRILL
She dyes: that sentence poisons her: O life!
What slaue would pledge a King in his owne wife?

CELESTINE
Welcome, ô poyson, phisicke against lust,
Thou holesome medicine to a constant bloud;
Thou rare Apothecary that canst keepe,
My chastity preseru'd, within this boxe;
Of tempting dust, this painted earthen pot,
That stands vpon the stall of the white soule,
To set the shop out like a flatterer,
To draw the customers of Sinne: come, come,
Thou art no poison, but a dyet-drinke,
To moderate my bloud: White-innocent Wine,
Art thou made guilty of my death? oh no,
For thou thy selfe art poison'd, take me hence,

For Innocence, shall murder Innocence.

Drinkes.

TERRILL
Holde, holde, thou shalt not dye, my Bride, my wife,
O stop that speedy messenger of death;
O let him not run downe that narrow path,
Which leades vnto thy heart; nor carry newes
To thy remoouing soule, that thou must dye.

CELESTINE
Tis done already, the Spirituall Court,
Is breaking vp; all Offices discharg'd,
My soule remooues from this weake standing house,
Of fraile mortallity; Deare Father, blesse
Me now and euer: Dearer Man, farewell,
I ioyntly take my leaue of thee and life,
Goe, tell the King thou hast a constant wife.

TERRILL
I had a constant wife, Ile tell the King;
Vntill the King—what dost thou smile? art thou
A Father?

SIR QUINTILIAN SHORTHOSE
Yea, smiles on my cheekes arise,
To see how sweetly a true virgin dyes.

Enter BLUNT, CRISPINUS, FANNIUS, PHILOCALIA, DICACHE, PETULA, lights before them.

CRISPINUS
Sir Walter Terrill, gallants are all ready?

TERRILL
All ready.

DEMETRIUS
Well said, come, come, wher's the Bride?

TERRILL
She's going to forbid the Banes agen.
She'll dye a maide: and see, she keeps her oath.

ALL THE MEN
Faire Cælestine!

LADIES

The Bride!

TERRILL
She that was faire,
Whom I cal'd faire and Cælestine.

OMNES
Dead!

SIR QUINTILIAN SHORTHOSE
Dead, sh's deathes Bride, he hath her maidenhead.

CRISPINUS
Sir Walter Terrill.

OMNEs
Tell vs how.

TERRILL
All cease,
The subiect that we treate of now is Peace,
If you demaund how: I can tell: if why,
Aske the King that; he was the cause, not I.
Let it suffice, she's dead, she kept her vow,
Aske the King why, and then Ile tell you how:
Nay giue your Reuels life, tho she be gone,
To Court with all your preparation;
Leade on, and leade her on; if any aske
The mistery, say death presents a maske,
Ring peales of Musicke, you are Louers belles,
The losse of one heauen, brings a thousand hels.

Exeunt.

SCENE II. The King's Banquet Hall

Enter an arm'd Stewerd, after him the seruice of a Banquet: the KING at another doore meetes them,
they Exeunt.

KING
Why so, euen thus the Mercury of Heauen,
Vshers th' ambrosiate banquet of the Gods,
When a long traine of Angels in a ranke,
Serue the first course, and bow their Christall knees,
Before the Siluer table; where Ioues page
Sweet Ganimed filles Nectar: when the Gods

Drinke healthes to Kings, they pledge them; none but Kings
Dare pledge the Gods; none but Gods drinke to Kings.
Men of our house are we prepar'd?

Enter SERUANTS.

SERUANT
My Leige,
All waite the presence of the Bride.

KING
The Bride?
Yea, euery senceles thing, which she beholdes,
Will looke on her agen, her eyes reflection,
Will make the walles all eyes, with her perfection:
Obserue me now, because of Maskes and Reuels,
And many nuptiall ceremonies: Marke,
This I create the Presence, heere the State,
Our Kingdomes seate, shall sit in honours Pride,
Like pleasures Queene, there will I place the Bride:
Be gone, be speedy, let me see it done.

Exeunt.

A King in Loue, is Steward to himselfe,
And neuer scornes the office, my selfe buy,
All glances from the Market of her eye.

Soft Musicke, chaire is set vnder a Canopie.

KING
Sound Musicke, thou sweet suiter to the ayre,
Now wooe the ayre agen, this is the houre,
Writ in the Calender of time, this houre,
Musicke shall spend, the next and next the Bride;
Her tongue will read the Musicke-Lecture: Wat
I loue thee Wat, because thou art not wise;
Not deep-read in the volume of a man,
Thou neuer sawst a thought, poore soule thou thinkst,
The heart and tongue is cut out of one peece,
But th'art deceau'd, the world hath a false light,
Fooles thinke tis day, when wise men know tis night.

Enter SIR QUINTILIAN SHORT HOSE.

SIR QUINTILIAN SHORTHOSE
My Leige, they're come, a maske of gallants.

KING
Now—the spirit of Loue vshers my bloud.

SIR QUINTILIAN SHORTHOSE
They come.
The Watch-word in a Maske is the bolde Drum.

Enter BLUNT, CRISPINUS, DEMETRIUS, PHILOCALIA, PETULA, DICACHE, all maskt, two and two with lights
like maskers: CELESTINE in a chaire.

TERRILL
All pleasures guard my King, I heere present,
My oath vpon the knee of duety: knees
Are made for Kings, they are the subiects Fees.

KING
Wat Terrill, th'art ill suited, ill made vp,
In Sable collours, like a night peece dyed,
Com'st thou the Prologue of a Maske in blacke;
Thy body is ill shapt; a Bride-groome too
Looke how the day is drest in Siluer cloth,
Laide round about with golden Sunne-beames: so
(As white as heauen) should a fresh Bride-groome goe.
What? Cælestine the Bride, in the same taske?
Nay then I see ther's mistery in this maske,
Prethee resolue me Wat?

TERRILL
My gracious Lord,
That part is hers, she actes it; onely I
Present the Prologue, she the misterie.

KING
Come Bride, the Sceane of blushing entred first,
Your cheekes are setled now, and past the worst;

Vnmasks her.

A mistery? oh none plaies heere but death,
This is deaths motion, motionles? speake you,
Flatter no longer; thou her Bride-groome; thou
Her Father speake.

SIR QUINTILIAN SHORTHOSE
Dead.

TERRILL
Dead.

KING
How?

SIR QUINTILIAN SHORTHOSE
Poyson'd.

KING
And poyson'd?
What villaine durst blaspheme her beauties, or
Prophane the cleare religion of her eyes?

TERRILL
Now King I enter, now the Sceane is mine,
My tongue is tipt with poison; know who speakes,
And looke into my thoughts; I blush not King,
To call thee Tyrant: death hath set my face,
And made my bloud bolde; heare me spirits of men,
And place your eares vpon your hearts; the day
(The fellow to this night) saw her and me,
Shake hands together: for the booke of heauen,
Made vs eternall friends: thus, Man and Wife,
This man of men (the King) what are not kings?
Was my chiefe guest, my royall guest, his Grace
Grac'd all the Table, and did well become
The vpper end, where sate my Bride: in briefe,
He tainted her chaste eares; she yet vnknowne,
His breath was treason, tho his words were none.
Treason to her and me, he dar'd me then,
(Vnder the couert of a flattering smile,)
To bring her where she is, not as she is,
Aliue for lust, not dead for (Chastity:
The resolution of my soule, out-dar'd,)
I swore and taxt my faith with a sad oath;
Which I maintaine; heere take her, she was mine,
When she was liuing, but now dead, she's thine.

KING
Doe not confound me quite; for mine owne guilt,
Speakes more within me then thy tongue containes;
Thy sorrow is my shame: yet heerein springs,
Ioy out of sorrow, boldnes out of shame;
For I by this haue found, once in my life,
A faithfull subiect, thou a constant wife.

CELESTINE
A constant wife.

KING
Am I confounded twice?
Blasted with wonder.

TERRILL
O delude we not,
Thou art too true to liue agen, too faire
To be my Cælestine, too constant farre
To be a woman.

CELESTINE
Not to be thy wife,
But first I pleade my duetie, and salute
The world agen.

SIR QUINTILIAN SHORTHOSE
My King, my Sonne, know all,
I am an Actor in this misterie,
And beare the chiefest part. The Father I,
Twas I that ministred to her chaste bloud,
A true somniferous potion, which did steale
Her thoughts to sleepe, and flattered her with death:
I cal'd it a quick poison'd drug, to trie
The Bride-groomes loue, and the Brides constancie.
He in the passion of his loue did fight,
A combat with affection; so did both,
She for the poison stroue, he for his oath:
Thus like a happie Father, I haue won,
A constant Daughter, and a louing Sonne.

KING
Mirrour of Maidens, wonder of thy name,
I giue thee that art giuen, pure, chaste, the same
Heere Wat: I would not part (for the worlds pride)
So true a Bride-groome, and so chaste a Bride.

CRISPINUS
My Leige, to wed a Comicall euent,
To presupposed tragicke Argument:
Vouchsafe to exercise your eyes, and see
A humorous dreadfull Poet take degree.

KING
Dreadfull in his proportion or his pen?

CRISPINUS
In both, he calles himselfe the whip of men.

KING
If a cleare merrit stand vpon his praise,
Reach him a Poets Crowne (the honour'd Bayes)
But if he claime it, wanting right thereto,
(As many bastard Sonnes of Poesie doe)
Race downe his vsurpation to the ground.
True Poets are with Arte and Nature Crown'd.
But in what molde so ere this man bee cast;
We make him thine Crispinus, wit and iudgement,
Shine in thy numbers, and thy soule I know,
Will not goe arm'd in passion gainst thy foe:
Therefore be thou our selfe; whilst our selfe sit,
But as spectator of this Sceane of wit.

CRISPINUS
Thankes royall Lord, for these high honors done,
To me vnworthie, my mindes brightest fires
Shall all consume them selues, in purest flame,
On the Alter of your deare eternall name.

KING
Not vnder vs, but next vs take thy Seate,
Artes nourished by Kings make Kings more great,
Vse thy Authority.

CRISPINUS
Demetrius.
Call in that selfe-creating Horace, bring
Him and his shaddow foorth.

DEMETRIUS
Both shall appeare,
o black-eyed star must sticke in vertues Spheare.

Enter SIR VAUGHAN.

SIR VAUGHAN
Ounds did you see him, I pray let all his Masesties most excellent dogs, be set at liberties, and haue their freedoms to smell him out.

DEMETRIUS
Smell whom?

SIR VAUGHAN
Whom? The Composer, the Prince of Poets, Horace, Horace, he's departed: in Gods name and the Kinges I sarge you to ring it out from all our eares, for Horaces bodie is departed: Master hue and crie shall—God blesse King Williams, I crie you mercy and aske forgiuenes, for mine eyes did not finde in their hearts to looke vppon your Masestie.

KING
What news with thee Sir Vaughan?

SIR VAUGHAN
Newes? God tis as vrse newes as I can desire to bring about mee: our vnhansome-fac'd Poet does play at bo-peepes with your Grace, and cryes all-hidde as boyes doe.

OFFICERS
Stand by, roome there, backe, roome for the Poet.

SIR VAUGHAN
He's reprehended and taken, by Sesu I reioyce very neere as much as if I had discouer'd a New-found Land, or the North and East Indies.

Enter TUCCA his boy after him with two pictures vnder his cloake, and a wreath of nettles: HORACE and ASINIUS BUBO pul'd in by th' hornes bound both like Satyres, SIR ADAM following, MISTRIS MINIVER with him, wearing Tuccaes chaine.

TUCCA
So, tug, tug, pull the mad Bull in by'th hornes: So, baite one at that stake my place-mouth yelpers, and one at that stake Gurnets-head.

KING
What busie fellow's this?

TUCCA
Saue thee, my most gracious King a Harts saue thee, all hats and caps are thine, and therefore I vaile: for but to thee great Sultane Soliman, I scorne to be thus put off or to deliuer vp this sconce I wud.

KING
Sir Vaughan, what's this iolly Captaines name?

SIR VAUGHAN
Has a very sufficient name, and is a man has done God and his Country as good and as hot Seruice (in conquering this vile Monster-Poet) as euer did S. George his horse-backe about the Dragon.

TUCCA
I sweate for't, but Tawsoone, holde thy tongue, Mon Dieu, if thou't praise mee, doo't behinde my backe: I am my weighty Soueraigne one of thy graines, thy valliant vassaile; aske not what I am, but read, turne ouer, vnclaspe thy Chronicles: there thou shalt finde Buffe-Ierkin; there read my points of war; I am one a thy Mandilian-Leaders; one that enters into thy royall bands for thee; Pantilius Tucca; one of thy Kingdomes chiefest quarrellers; one a thy most faithfull—fy—fy—fy—

SIR VAUGHAN
Drunkerds I holde my life.

TUCCA

No whirligig, one of his faithfull fighters; thy drawer ô royall Tamor Cham.

SIR VAUGHAN
Goe too, I pray Captaine Tucca, giue vs all leaue to doe our busines before the King.

TUCCA
With all my heart, shi, shi, shi shake that Beare-whelp when thou wut.

SIR VAUGHAN
Horace and Bubo, pray send an answere into his Masesties eares, why you goe thus in Ouids Morter-Morphesis and strange fashions of apparrell.

TUCCA
Cur why?

ASINIUS BUBO
My Lords, I was drawne into this beastly suite by head and shoulders onely for loue I bare to my Ningle.

TUCCA
Speake Ningle, thy mouth's next, belch out, belch, why—

HORACE
I did it to retyre me from the world;
And turne my Muse into a Timonist,
Loathing the general Leprozie of Sinne,
Which like a plague runs through the soules of men:
I did it but to—

TUCCA
But to bite euery Motley-head vice by'th nose, you did it Ningle to play the Bug-beare Satyre, & make a Campe royall of fashion-mongers quake at your paper Bullets; you Nastie Tortois, you and your Itchy Poetry breake out like Christmas, but once a yeare, and then you keepe a Reuelling, & Araigning, & a Scratching of mens faces, as tho you were Tyber the long-tail'd Prince of Rattes, doe you?

CRISPINUS
Horace.

SIR VAUGHAN
Silence, pray let all vrdes be strangled, or held fast betweene your teeth.

CRISPINUS
Vnder controule of my dreade Soueraigne,
We are thy Iudges; thou that didst Arraigne,
Art now prepar'd for condemnation;
Should I but bid thy Muse stand to the Barre,
Thy selfe against her wouldst giue euidence:
For flat rebellion gainst the Sacred lawes
Of diuine Poesie: heerein most she mist,

Thy pride and scorne made her turne Saterist,
And not her loue to vertue (as thou Preachest)
Or should we minister strong pilles to thee:
What lumpes of hard and indigested stuffe,
Of bitter Satirisme, of Arrogance,
Of Selfe-loue, of Detraction, of a blacke
And stinking Insolence should we fetch vp?
But none of these, we giue thee what's more fit,
With stinging nettles Crowne his stinging wit.

TUCCA
Wel said my Poeticall huckster, now he's in thy handling rate him, doe rate him well.

HORACE
O I beseech your Maiesty, rather then thus to be netled, Ile ha my Satyres coate pull'd ouer mine eares, and bee turn'd out a the nine Muses Seruice.

ASINIUS BUBO
And I too, let mee be put to my shiftes with myne Ningle.

SIR VAUGHAN
By Sesu so you shall M. Bubo; flea off this hairie skin
M. Horace, so, so, so, vntrusse, vntrusse.

TUCCA
His Poeticall wreath my dapper puncke-fetcher.

HORACE
Ooh—

SIR VAUGHAN
Nay your oohs, nor your Callin-oes cannot serue your turne; your tongue you know is full of blisters with rayling, your face full of pockey-holes and pimples, with your fierie inuentions: and therefore to preserue your head from aking, this Biggin is yours,—nay by Sesu you shall bee a Poet, though not Lawrefyed, yet Nettlefyed, so:

TUCCA
Sirra stincker, thou'rt but vntruss'd now, I owe thee a whipping still, and Ile pay it: I haue layde roddes in Pisse and Vineger for thee: It shall not bee the Whipping a' th Satyre, nor the Whipping of the blinde-Beare, but of a counterfeit Iugler, that steales the name of Horace.

KING
How? counterfeit? does hee vsurpe that name?

SIR VAUGHAN
Yes indeede ant please your Grace, he does sup vp that abhominable name.

TUCCA

Hee does O King Cambises, hee does: thou hast no part of Horace in thee but's name, and his damnable vices: thou hast such a terrible mouth, that thy beard's afraide to peepe out: but, looke heere you staring Leuiathan, heere's the sweete visage of Horace; looke perboylde-face, looke; Horace had a trim long-beard, and a reasonable good face for a Poet, (as faces goe now-a-dayes) Horace did not skrue and wriggle himselfe into great Mens famyliarity, (impudentlie) as thou doost: nor weare the Badge of Gentlemens company, as thou doost thy Taffetie sleeues tackt too onely with some pointes of profit: No, Horace had not his face puncht full of Oylet-holes, like the couer of a warming-pan: Horace lou'd Poets well, and gaue Coxcombes to none but fooles; but thou lou'st none, neither Wisemen nor fooles, but thy selfe: Horace was a goodly Corpulent Gentleman, and not so leane a hollow-cheekt Scrag as thou art: No, heere's thee Coppy of thy countenance, by this will I learne to make a number of villanous faces more, and to looke scuruily vpon'th world, as thou dost.

CRISPINUS
Sir Vaughan will you minister their oath?

SIR VAUGHAN
Master Asinius Bubo, you shall sweare as little as you can, one oath shall damme vp your Innocent mouth.

ASINIUS BUBO
Any oath Sir, Ile sweare any thing.

SIR VAUGHAN
You shall sweare, by Phœbus (who is your Poets good Lord and Master,) that heere-after you will not hyre Horace, to giue you poesies for rings, or hand-kerchers, or kniues which you vnderstand not, nor to write your Loue-letters; which you (in turning of a hand) set your markes vpon, as your owne: nor you shall not carry Lattin Poets about you, till you can write and read English at most; and lastlye that you shall not call Horace your Ningle.

ASINIUS BUBO
By Phœbus I sweare all this, and as many oathes as you will, so I may trudge.

SIR VAUGHAN
Trudge then, pay your legs for Fees, and bee dissarg'd.

TUCCA
Tprooth—runne Red-cap, ware hornes there.

Exit ASINIUS BUBO

SIR VAUGHAN
Now Master Horace, you must be a more horrible swearer, for 'your oath must be (like your wittes) of many collours; and like a Brokers booke of many parcels.

TUCCA
Read, read; th'inuentory of his oath.

HORACE

Ile sweare till my haire stands vp an end, to bee rid of this sting, oh this sting!

SIR VAUGHAN
Tis not your sting of conscience, is it?

TUCCA
Vpon him: Inprimis.

SIR VAUGHAN
Inprimis, you shall sweare by Phœbus and the halfe a score Muses lacking one: not to sweare to hang
your selfe, if you thought any Man, Ooman or Silde, could write Playes and Rimes, as
well-fauour'd ones as your selfe.

TUCCA
Well sayd, hast brought him toth gallowes already?

SIR VAUGHAN
You shall sweare not to bumbast out a new Play, with the olde lynings of Iestes, stolne from the Temples
Reuels.

TUCCA
To him olde Tango.

SIR VAUGHAN
Moreouer, you shall not sit in a Gallery, when your Comedies and Enterludes haue entred their Actions,
and there make vile and bad faces at euerie lyne, to make Sentlemen haue an eye to you, and to make
Players afraide to take your part.

TUCCA
Thou shalt be my Ningle for this.

SIR VAUGHAN
Besides, you must forsweare to venter on the stage, when your Play is ended, and to exchange
curtezies, and complements with Gallants in the Lordes roomes, to make all the house rise vp in Armes,
and to cry that's Horace, that's he, that's he, that's he, that pennes and purges Humours and diseases.

TUCCA
There boy, agen.

SIR VAUGHAN
Secondly, when you bid all your friends to the marriage of a poore couple, that is to say: your Wits and
necessities, alias dictus, to the rifling of your Muse: alias, your Muses vp-sitting: alias a Poets Whitson-
Ale; you shall sweare that within three days after, you shall not abroad, in Booke-binders shops, brag
that your Vize-royes or Tributorie-Kings, haue done homage to you, or paide quarterage.

TUCCA
Ile busse thy head Holofernes.

SIR VAUGHAN
Moreouer and Inprimis, when a Knight or Sentlemen of vrship, does giue you his passe-port, to trauaile in and out to his Company, and giues you money for Gods sake; I trust in Sesu, you will sweare (tooth and nayle) not to make scalde and wry-mouth Iestes vpon his Knight-hood, will you not?

HORACE
I neuer did it by Parnassus.

TUCCA
Wut sweare by Parnassus and lye too, Doctor Doddipol?

SIR VAUGHAN
Thirdly, and last of all sauing one, when your Playes are misse-likt at Court, you shall not crye Mew like a Pusse-cat, and say you are glad you write out of the Courtiers Element.

TUCCA
Let the Element alone, tis out a thy reach.

SIR VAUGHAN
In brieflynes, when you Sup in Tauernes, amongst your betters, you shall sweare not to dippe your Manners in too much sawce, nor at Table to fling Epigrams, Embleames, or Play-speeches about you (lyke Hayle-stones) to keepe you out of the terrible daunger of the Shot, vpon payne to sit at the vpper ende of the Table, a'th left hand of Carlo Buffon: sweare all this, by Apollo and the eight or nine Muses.

HORACE
By Apollo, Helicon, the Muses (who march three and three in a rancke) and by all that belongs to Pernassus, I sweare all this.

TUCCA
Beare witnes.

CRISPINUS
That fearefull wreath, this honour is your due,
All Poets shall be Poet-Apes but you;
Thankes (Learnings true Mecænas, Poesies king)
Thankes for that gracious eare, which you haue lent,
To this most tedious, most rude argument.

KING
Our spirits haue well beene feasted; he whose pen
Drawes both corrupt, and cleare bloud from all men:
(Careles what veine he prickes) let him not raue,
When his owne sides are strucke, blowes, blowes, doe craue.

TUCCA
Kings-truce, my noble Hearbe-a-grace; my Princely sweet-William,
a boone—Stay first, Ist a match or no match, Lady Furniuall Ist?

SIR ADRIAN & SIR QUINTILIAN SHORTHOSE
A match?

MISTRESS MINIVER
I, a match, since he hath hit the Mistris so often I'th
fore-game, we'll eene play out a rubbers.

SIR ADAM
Take her for me.

SIR QUINTILIAN SHORTHOSE
Take her for thy selfe, not for me.

SIR VAUGHAN
Play out your rubbers in Gods name, by Sesu Ile neuer
boule more in your Alley, Iddow.

SIR QUINTILIAN SHORTHOSE
My Chaine.

SIR ADAM
My Purse.

TUCCA
Ile Chaine thee presently, and giue thee ten pound and a purse: a boone my Leige: ... daunce ô my
delicate Rufus, at my wedding with this reuerend Antiquary; ist done? wut thou?

KING
Ile giue thee Kingly honour: Night and Sleepe,
With silken Ribands would tye vp our eyes,
But Mistris Bride, one measure shall be led,
In scorne of Mid-nights hast, and then to bed.

Exeunt.

EPILOGUS

TUCCA
Gentlemen, Gallants, and you my little Swaggerers that fight lowe: my tough hearts of Oake that stand
too't so valliantly, and are still within a yard of your Capten: Now the Trumpets (that set men together
by the eares) haue left their Tantara-rag-boy, let's part friends. I recant, beare witnes all you Gentle-
folkes (that walke i'th Galleries) I recant the opinions which I helde of Courtiers, Ladies, & Cittizens,
when once (in an assembly of Friers) I railde vpon them: that Hereticall Libertine Horace, taught me so
to mouth it. Besides, twas when stiffe Tucca was a boy: twas not Tucca that railed and roar'd then, but
the Deuill & his Angels: But now, Kings-truce, the Capten Summons a parlee, and deliuers himselfe and
his prating company into your hands, vpon what composition you wil. Are you pleas'd? and Ile dance

Friskin for ioy, but if you be not, by'th Lord Ile see you all—heere for your two pence a peice agen, before Ile loose your company. I know now some be come hyther with cheekes swolne as big with hisses, as if they had the tooth-ach: vds-foote, if I stood by them, Ide bee so bold as—intreate them to hisse in another place. Are you aduiz'd what you doe when you hisse? you blowe away Horaces reuenge: but if you set your hands and Seales to this, Horace will write against it, and you may haue more sport: he shall not loose his labour, he shall not turne his blanke verses into wast paper: No, my Poetasters will not laugh at him, but will vntrusse him agen, and agen, and agen. Ile tell you what you shall doe, cast your little Tucca into a Bell: doe, make a Bell of me, and be al you my clappers, vpon condition, wee may haue a lustie peale, this colde weather: I haue but two legs left me, and they are both yours: Good night my two penny Tenants God night.

FINIS.

Thomas Dekker – A Short Biography

Thomas Dekker was born around 1572, there is no certainty as to date and it is only probable that he was born in London. Little is known of his early years. From such an unknown start he was however to make quite a name for himself.

By the mid 1590s Dekker had set forth on a career as a playwright. Samples of his work (though not the actual date) can be found in the manuscript of Sir Thomas More. Of more certainty is work as a playwright for the Admiral's Men of Philip Henslowe, in whose records of account he is first mentioned in early 1598.

While there are plays connected with his name performed as early as 1594, it is not clear that he was the original author or part of a team involved in revising and updating. Much of his work has been lost and whilst his prolific output argues against any uniform quality there are undoubted gems both as a solo writer and as part of various collaborations. Indeed between 1598 and 1602, about forty plays for Henslowe, usually in collaboration, can be attributed to him.

Dekker's name first appears in Henslowe's diary* in connection with "fayeton" (presumably, Phaeton) in 1598. There follow, before 1599, payments for work on The Triplicity of Cuckolds, The Mad Man's Morris, and Hannibal and Hermes. He worked on these plays with Robert Wilson, Henry Chettle, and Michael Drayton. With Drayton, he also worked on history plays on the French civil wars, Earl Godwin, and others.

It is also recorded at this time that Dekker's long association with financial mishaps was going to be a life-long concern. He was imprisoned for a short time for debt in Poultry Compter, a small prison run by the Sherriff of London. It was used to house prisoners such as vagrants, debtors and religious dissenters, as well as criminals convicted of misdemeanours including homosexuality, prostitution and drunkenness.

In 1599, he wrote plays on Troilus and Cressida, Agamemnon (with Chettle), and Page of Plymouth. In that year, also, he collaborated with Chettle, Jonson, and Marston on a play about Robert II.

1599 also saw the production of three plays that have survived including his most famous work, The Shoemaker's Holiday, or the Gentle Craft. This play reflects the daily lives of ordinary Londoners, and contains the poem The Merry Month of May. The play reflects the trend for the intermingling of everyday subjects with the fantastical, embodied here by the rise of a craftsman to Mayor and the involvement of an unnamed but idealised king in the concluding banquet. Old Fortunatus and Patient Grissel are the two other surviving plays.

In 1600, he worked on The Seven Wise Masters, Fortune's Tennis, Cupid and Psyche, and Fair Constance of Rome. The next year, in addition to the classic Satiromastix, he worked on a play possibly about Sebastian of Portugal and Blurt, Master Constable, on which he may have collaborated with Thomas Middleton.

To these years also belong the collaborations with Ben Jonson and John Marston, which presumably contributed to the War of the Theatres in 1600 and 1601. To Jonson, Dekker was a hack, a "dresser of plays about town"; Jonson made fun of Dekker as Demetrius Fannius in Poetaster and as Anaides in Cynthia's Revels.

Dekker's riposte, Satiromastix, performed both by the Lord Chamberlain's Men and the child actors of Paul's, casts Jonson as an affected, hypocritical Horace and marks the end of the "poetomachia".

In 1602 he revised two older plays, Pontius Pilate (1597) and the second part of Sir John Oldcastle. He also collaborated on Caesar's Fall, Jephthah, A Medicine for a Curst Wife, Sir Thomas Wyatt (on Wyatt's rebellion), and Christmas Comes But Once a Year.

By 1603, Jonson and Dekker collaborated again, on a pageant for the Royal Entry, delayed from the coronation of James I, for which Dekker also wrote the festival book The Magnificent Entertainment.

At this point Dekker becomes more interested in writing pamphlets; he had done so from the start of his career but now increases his work flow and his playwriting output noticeably declines. It appears also that his association with Henslowe also breaks at this point.

In Dekker's first rush of pamphleteering, in 1603, was The Wonderful Year, a journalistic account of the death of Elizabeth, accession of James I, and the 1603 plague, that combined a wide variety of literary styles to convey the extraordinary events of that year ('wonderful' here meaning astonishing). Its reception prompted two more plague pamphlets, News From Gravesend and The Meeting of Gallants at an Ordinary. The Double PP (1606) is an anti-Catholic tract written in response to the Gunpowder Plot. News From Hell (1606) is an homage to and continuation of Nash's Pierce Penniless. The Seven Deadly Sins of London (1606) continues the plague pamphlet series.

In 1604, he and Middleton wrote The Honest Whore for the Fortune, and Dekker contributed a sequel himself the following year. The Middleton/Dekker collaboration The Family of Love also dates from this time. Dekker and Webster also wrote Westward Ho and Northward Ho for Paul's Boys.

The failures of The Whore of Babylon (1607) and If This Be Not a Good Play, the Devil is in It (1611) left him crestfallen; the latter play was rejected by Prince Henry's Men before failing for Queen Anne's Men at the Red Bull Theatre.

After 1608, Dekker produced his most popular pamphlets: a series of "cony-catching" pamphlets that described the various tricks and deceits of confidence-men and thieves, including Thieves' Cant. These pamphlets, which Dekker often updated and reissued, include The Belman of London (1608, now The

Bellman of London), Lanthorne and Candle-light, Villainies Discovered by Candlelight, and English Villainies. They owe their form and many of their incidents to similar pamphlets by Robert Greene.

Other pamphlets are journalistic in form and offer vivid pictures of Jacobean London. The Dead Term (1608) describes Westminster during summer vacation. The Guls Horne-Booke (1609, now The Gull's Hornbook) describes the life of city gallants, with a valuable account of behaviour in the London theatres. Work for Armourers (1609) and The Artillery Garden (1616) (the latter in verse) describe aspects of England's military industries. London Look Back (1630) treats 1625, the year of James's death, while Wars, Wars, Wars (1628) describes European turmoil.

The Roaring Girl, a city comedy that using the real-life figure 'Moll Cutpurse', aka Mary Frith, was another collaboration with Middleton in 1611. The same year, he wrote another tragicomedy; Match Me in London.

In 1612, Dekker's lifelong problem with debt reached a crisis point when he was imprisoned in the King's Bench Prison on a debt of forty pounds to the father of John Webster. He remained there for seven years and continued writing pamphlets during these years but wrote no plays. He did however contribute six prison-based sketches to the sixth edition (1616) of Sir Thomas Overbury's Characters; and he revised Lanthorne and Candlelight to reflect what he had learned in prison.

Dekker also wrote a long poem Dekker His Dreame (1620) cataloguing his despairing confinement;

After his release, he collaborated with Day on Guy of Warwick (1620), The Wonder of a Kingdom (1623), and The Bellman of Paris (1623). He also wrote the tragicomedy The Noble Spanish Soldier (1622) and later reworked material from this play into a comedic form to produce The Welsh Ambassador (1623).

With John Ford, he wrote The Sun's Darling (1624), The Fairy Knight (1624), and The Bristow Merchant (1624).

Another play, The Late Murder of the Son upon the Mother, or Keep the Widow Waking (with Ford, Webster, and William Rowley) dramatized two recent murders in Whitechapel, and resulted in a suit for slander heard in the Star Chamber.

Dekker turned once more to pamphlet-writing, revamping old work and writing a new preface to his most popular tract, The Bellman of London.

Dekker's plays of the 1620s were staged at the large amphitheaters on the north side of London, most commonly at the Red Bull; only two of his later plays were seen at the more exclusive, indoor Cockpit Theatre. The Shoreditch amphitheaters had become identified with the louder, less reputable play-goers, such as apprentices. Dekker's type of play seems to have suited them perfectly. Full of bold action and complementary to the values and beliefs of such audiences, his drama carried much of the thrusting optimism of Elizabethan drama into the Caroline era.

Dekker published no more work after 1632, and he it is thought he died on August 25th, 1632, recorded as "Thomas Dekker, householder". He is buried at St. James's in Clerkenwell.

Most of Dekker's work is lost. His disordered life, and his lack of a firm connection (such as Shakespeare had) with a single company, may have hindered the preservation or publication of manuscripts although perhaps twenty of his plays were published during his lifetime.

Henslowe's diary

Philip Henslowe was an Elizabethan theatrical entrepreneur and impresario although he had a wide range of other business interests. Henslowe's reputation rests on the survival of his diary, a primary source for information about the theatrical world of Renaissance London.

Henslowe's "diary" is a valuable source on the theatrical history of the period. It is a collection of memoranda and notes that record payments to writers, box office takings, and lists of money lent. Also of interest are records of the purchase of expensive costumes and of stage properties, such as the dragon in Christopher Marlowe's Doctor Faustus, providing an insight into the staging of plays in the Elizabethan theatre.

The diary is written on the reverse of pages of a book of accounts of his brother-in-law Ralf Hogge's ironworks, kept by his brother John Henslowe for the period 1576–1581. Hogge was the Queen's Gunstone maker, and produced both iron cannon and shot for the Royal Armouries at the Tower of London. John Henslowe seems to have acted as his agent, and Philip to have prudently reused his old account book. Hence these entries are also a valuable source for the early iron-making industry.

The diary begins with Henslowe's theatrical activities for 1592. Entries, with varying degrees of detail (authors' names were not included before 1597), until 1609. In the years before his death, Henslowe appears to have run his theatrical interests from a greater distance.

The diary records payments to twenty-seven Elizabethan playwrights. He variously commissioned, bought and produced plays by, or made loans to Ben Jonson, Christopher Marlowe, Thomas Middleton, Robert Greene, Henry Chettle, George Chapman, Thomas Dekker, John Webster, Anthony Munday, Henry Porter, John Day, John Marston and Michael Drayton. The diary reveals the varying partnerships between writers, in an age when many plays were collaborations. It also shows Henslowe to have been a careful man of business, obtaining security in the form of rights to his authors' works, and holding their manuscripts, while tying them to him with loans and advances. If a play was successful, Henslowe would commission a sequel.

Performances of works with titles similar to Shakespearean plays, such as a Hamlet, a Henry VI, Part 1, a Henry V, a The Taming of the Shrew and a Titus Andronicus are mentioned in the diary with no author listed. Most of these plays were recorded when the Admiral's Men and the Lord Chamberlain's Men briefly joined forces when the playhouses were closed owing to the plague (June 1594).

In 1599, Henslowe paid Dekker and Henry Chettle for a play called Troilus and Cressida, which is probably the play currently known as British Museum MS. Add 10449 (the actors' names that appear in the plot connect it to the Admiral's Men and date it between March 1598 and July 1600). There is no mention of William Shakespeare (or for that matter Richard Burbage) in Henslowe's diary (despite the forgeries of John Payne Collier), this is due to the fact that Shakespeare and Burbage were during most of their career not connected to Henslowe's theatre, Shakespeare's company, the Lord Chamberlain's Men, performed at The Theatre (starting in 1594) and later The Globe Theatre (starting in 1599).

Thomas Dekker – A Concise Bibliography

Plays – Sole Authorship
The Shoemaker's Holiday (1599)
Old Fortunatus (1600)
The Noble Spanish Soldier (1602)
Troja-Nova Triumphans, or London Triumphing (1612)
London's Tempe; or, The Feild of Happines (1629)
The Honest Whore, Part II (1630)
Match Me in London (1631)
The Wonder of a Kingdom (1634)

Plays – Co-Written
Satiro-Mastix (1601) with Marston
Blurt, Master Constable (1602) with Middleton
Patient Grissill (1603) with Chettle and Haughton
The Honest Whore, Part I (1604) with Middleton
The Magnificent Entertainment (1604) with Jonson et al.
The Family of Love (1603-1607) with Middleton
Northward Ho (1607) with Webster
Westward Ho (1607) with Webster
The Famous History of Sir Thomas Wyatt (1607) with Webster
The Roaring Girl (1610) with Middleton
The Witch of Edmonton (1621) with Ford, Rowley, &c.
The Virgin-Martyr (1622) with Massinger
The Sun's Darling (1623-4) with Ford
The Bloody Banquet (1639) with Middleton

Non-Dramatic Works
The Wonderful Year (1603)
News from Hell (1606)
The Double PP (1606)
The Seven Deadly Sins of London (1606)
Jests to Make You Merry (1607)
The Bellman of London (1608)
Lanthorne and Candle-light (1608)
The Dead Term (1608)
The Gull's Hornbook (1609)
The Four Birds of Noah's Ark (1609)
The Raven's Almanack (1609)
Work for Armourers (1609)
O Per Se O (1612)
A Strange Horse-Race (1613)
Dekker, His Dreame (1620)
A Rod for Runaways (1625)

Poems
Golden Slumbers Kiss Your Eyes
Beauty Arise
Cast Away Care
The Invitation
Fancies Are But Streams
Here Lies The Blithe Spring

Printed in Great Britain
by Amazon

17452862R00054